RALPH STORER is an experienced and respected hillwalker who has hiked and backpacked extensively around the world. Despite being a Sassenach by birth, he has lived in Scotland since studying psychology at Dundee University and has a great affinity for the Highlands, where he can be seen in all weathers roaming the glens and tramping the tops. As well as disappearing into the hills for a regular fix of nature, he also writes novels and sexological non-fiction, and produces darkwave music on his home computer.

The Ultimate Guide to the Munros, Volume 1: Southern Highlands is the first volume in a series that draws on his decades of adventures in the Scottish Highlands.

This is a truly indispensible guide for the Munro-bagger. Bursting with information, wit and a delightful irreverence rarely found in this type of guide, it's a joy to read. Ralph and his motley crew are the perfect companions on a great day out. An absolute gem!
ALEX MacKINNON, Manager, Waterstone's George Street, Edinburgh

The Ultimate Guide to the Munros *picks up where others – including my own – leave off, with lots of nitty-gritty information on alternative routes, levels of difficulty and aids to navigation, all in a very up-beat style. Given that all this extra Munro-info would fill a gigantic Bumper Fun Book of the Munros, Ralph has chosen to break the list down into volumes, of which the Southern Highlands is the first... I look forward to seeing the rest of his fun-packed Munros series.* CAMERON MCNEISH, THE GREAT OUTDOORS

Fabulously illustrated... Entertaining as well as informative... One of the definitive guides to the Munros. PRESS & JOURNAL

BY THE SAME AUTHOR:

100 Best Routes on Scottish Mountains (Warner Books)
50 Best Routes on Skye and Raasay (Warner Books)
Exploring Scottish Hill Tracks (Warner Books)
The Joy of Hillwalking (Luath Press)
Mountain Trivia Challenge (Cordee)
The World's Great Adventure Treks (contributor) (New Holland)
Trekking Atlas of the World (contributor) (New Holland)
The Rumpy Pumpy Quiz Book (Metro Publishing)
Love Scenes (a novel) (Mercat)
50 Classic Routes on Scottish Mountains (Luath Press)

The Ultimate Guide to the Munros

Volume 1: Southern Highlands

RALPH STORER

Boot-tested and compiled by
The Go-Take-a-Hike Mountaineering Club

Luath Press Limited
EDINBURGH
www.luath.co.uk

For Christine

First published 2008
Reprinted 2009 with minor changes

ISBN (10): 1-906307-57-1
ISBN (13): 978-1-906307-57-8

The paper used in this book is recyclable. It is made from low-chlorine pulps produced in a low-energy, low-emission manner from renewable forests.

Printed and bound by Bell and Bain Ltd., Glasgow

Typeset in Tahoma by Ralph Storer

All maps reproduced by permission of Ordnance Survey on behalf of HMSO. © Crown copyright 2009. All rights reserved. Ordnance Survey Licence number 100016659.

Front cover artwork by Sinéad Bracken

All photographs by the author, including front cover (An Stuc north ridge), except those on pages 79, 84, 115, 130, 157, 164, 168, 213 & 219 by Allan Leighton.

CONTENTS

INTRODUCTION

The Go-Take-a-Hike Mountaineering Club

Ralph Storer President

Compiler of routes, penner of words, stopper of bucks, all-round good egg. His packed lunch of choice: Marjorie Seedlings plum jam sannies.

GiGi Custodian of the Common Sense

Farer (fairer?) of the Ways, arbiter of disputes, friend to all. Named after the two embarrassing Grooves occasioned by too much fence-sitting. Her packed lunch of choice: it depends.

F-Stop Controller of the Camera

Advisor of the Aperture. Recorder of the Ridiculous. So-named because he's always f***ing stopping to take photographs. His packed lunch of choice: ginger snaps.

Needlepoint Companion of the Compass

Wary Watcher of the Weather. Finds featureless plateaus intimidating, doesn't understand GPS, barely understands a compass. Her packed lunch of choice: fettuccini swirls.

Committee Members

Chilly Willy   Keeper of the Cool

AKA Snowballs. Peely-wally, estivates during summer, has never seen a midge, likes his toast crisp and even. His packed lunch of choice: freeze-dried ice-cream.

Torpedo   Expender of the Energy

Bald and streamlined. Loather of laziness. Scorch marks on boots. Ascends as fast as a falling Munro bagger descends. His packed lunch of choice: hi-energy nutrition bars.

Terminator   Raveller of the Rope

Grizzled, monosyllabic, self-taught suicide commando. Hater of the horizontal. Measures his life in scars. His packed lunch of choice: doesn't need lunch, lives on air.

Baffies   Entertainments Convenor

Allergic to exertion, prone to lassitude, suffers from altitude sickness above 600m, blisters easily, bleeds readily. His packed lunch of choice: triple chocolate layer cake.

Route Quality Ratings

*****   ## Outstanding

The best. Outstanding routes in every respect. The reason we climb mountains. The stuff of memories.

****   ## Excellent

Still great, but just lacking that extra something that would make them outstanding.

***   ## Very Good

Maybe not the best, but still commendable, perhaps outstanding or excellent in parts.

**   ## Good

Nothing to prise the uninitiated off the couch, yet still good enough to provide a satisfying hillwalk that brings a smile to the visage.

*   ## Fair

Could be better, but all Munros are worth booting up for, aren't they?

Route Rage Alert

Flagged on routes where 'challenging' terrain makes a beach holiday seem not such a bad idea after all.

Route Difficulty Grades

G1   **Mostly good going**

Mainly on good paths or good terrain. There may be occasional steep or rough sections, but not for long.

G2   **Appreciable awkward going**

Notably rough or steep terrain, perhaps prolonged, but not involving handwork on rock.

G3   **Minor handwork required**

Use of hands required on rock, e.g. for balance or a step-up, but not difficult or prolonged enough to constitute scrambling.

G4   **Easy scramble**

Includes one or more sections that require movement on rock with good holds.

G5   **Hard scramble**

One grade below a rock climb for which a rope would normally be required. Compared to G4, holds are often smaller and exposure is often greater.

OF MOUNTAINS AND MUNROS

It's a big place, the Scottish Highlands. It contains so many mountains that even resident hillwalkers struggle to climb them all in a lifetime. How many mountains? That depends...

If two summits 100m apart are separated by a shallow dip, do they constitute two mountains or one mountain with two tops? If the latter, then exactly how far apart do they have to be, and how deep does the intervening dip have to be, before they become two separate mountains?

Sir Hugh Munro (1856–1919), the third President of the Scottish Mountaineering Club, tackled this problem when he published his 'Tables of Heights over 3000 Feet' in the 1891 edition of the SMC Journal. Choosing the criterion of 3000ft in the imperial system of measurement as his cut-off point, he counted 283 separate Mountains and a further 255 Tops that were over 3000ft but not sufficiently separated from a Mountain to be considered separate Mountains themselves.

In a country whose vertical axis ranges from 0ft to 4409ft (1344m) at the summit of Ben Nevis, the choice of 3000ft as a cut-off point is aesthetically justifiable and gives a satisfying number of Mountains. A metric cut-off point of 1000m (3280ft), giving a more humble 137 Mountains, has never captured the hillgoing imagination.

Unfortunately Sir Hugh omitted to leave to posterity the criteria he used to distinguish Mountains from Tops, and Tops from other highpoints over 3000ft. In his notes to the Tables he even broached the impossibility of ever making definitive distinctions. Consider, for example, the problem of differentiating between Mountains, Tops and other highpoints on the

This irresistible invitation will be found near the start of one of the routes in this book.

Sir Hugh Munro himself never became a Munroist (someone who has climbed all the Munros). Of the Tables of the day, he climbed all but three: the Inaccessible Pinnacle (although that did not become a Munro until 1921), Carn an Fhidhleir and Carn Cloich-mhuilinn. The latter, which he was saving until last because it was close to his home, was ironically demoted to Top status in 1981.

Cairngorm plateaus, where every knoll surpasses 3000ft.

The Tables were a substantial achievement in an age when mapping of the Highlands was still rudimentary, but no sooner did they appear than their definitiveness become the subject of debate. In subsequent years Munro continued to fine-tune them, using new sources such as the Revised Six-inch Survey of the late 1890s. His notes formed the basis of a new edition of the Tables, published posthumously in 1921, which listed 276 separate Mountains (now known as Munros) and 267 Tops.

The 1921 edition also included J. Rooke Corbett's list of mountains with heights between 2500ft and 3000ft ('Corbetts'), and Percy Donald's list of hills in the Scottish Lowlands of 2000ft or over ('Donalds'). Corbett's test for a separate mountain was that it needed a re-ascent of 500ft (c150m) on all sides. Donald's test was more mathematical. A 'Donald' had to be 17 units from another one, where a unit was one twelfth of a mile (approx. one seventh of a kilometre) or one 50ft (approx. 15m) contour. We can assume that, however informally,

Munro used some similar formula concerning distance and height differential.

Over the years, various developments have conspired to prompt further amendments to the Tables, including metrication, improved surveying methods (most recently by satellite), and a desire on the part of each succeeding generation of editors to reduce what they have regarded as 'anomalies.' For example, the 'mountain range in miniature' of Beinn Eighe was awarded a second Munro in 1997 to redress the balance with similar but over-endowed multi-topped ridges such as the seven-Munro South Glen Shiel Ridge. Changes and the reasons for change are detailed individually in the main text (see Peak Fitness for details).

The first metric edition of the Tables in 1974 listed 279 Munros and 262 Tops. The 1981 edition listed 276 Munros and 240 Tops. The 1990 edition added an extra Munro. The current (1997) edition lists 284 Munros and 227 Tops. Watch this space.

BEN LOMOND

The first person to bag all the Munros may have been the Rev Archibald Robertson in 1901, although his notebooks bear no mention of him having climbed the Inaccessible Pinnacle and note that he gave up on Ben Wyvis to avoid a wetting.

The second Munroist was the Rev Ronald Burn, who additionally bagged all the Tops, in 1923, thus becoming the first 'Compleat Munroist' or Compleater. The third was James Parker, who additionally bagged all the Tops and Furths (the 3000ft summits of England, Wales and Ireland), in 1929. The latest edition of the Tables lists 1745 known Munroists.

THE SCOTTISH HIGHLANDS

The Scottish Highlands are characterised by a patchwork of mountains separated by deep glens, the result of glacial erosion in the distant past. On a global scale the mountains reach an insignificant height, topping out at (1344m/4409ft) on Ben Nevis. But in form they hold their own against any range in the world, many rising bold and beautiful from sea-level. For hillwalkers they

On Beinn Achaladair

have distinct advantages over higher mountain ranges: their height is ideal for day walks and glens give easy road access.

Moreover, the variety of mountain forms and landscapes is arguably greater than in any mountainous area of equivalent size. This is due to many factors, notably differing regional geology and the influence of the sea.

In an attempt to give some order to this complexity, the Highlands are traditionally divided into six regions, as detailed below. The potted overviews mislead in that they mask the variety within each region, ignore numerous exceptions to the rule and reflect road access as much as discernible regional boundaries, but they serve as introductory descriptions.

The Southern Highlands 46 Munros	Gentle, green and accessible, with scope for a great variety of mountain walks.
The Central Highlands 73 Munros	A combination of all the other regions, with some of the greatest rock faces in the country.
The Cairngorms 50 Munros	Great rolling plateaus, vast corries, remote mountain sanctuaries, sub-arctic ambience.
The Western Highlands 63 Munros	Dramatic landscapes, endless seascapes, narrow ridges, arrowhead peaks, rugged terrain.
The Northern Highlands 39 Munros	Massive, monolithic mountains rising out of a desolate, watery wilderness.
The Islands 13 Munros	Exquisite mountainscapes, knife-edge ridges, sky-high scrambling, maritime ambience.

THE SOUTHERN HIGHLANDS

The region covered by this guidebook, as its name implies, is the most southerly region in the Scottish Highlands. It is bounded on the west by the sea, on the east by the Tay Valley (the A9 Perth – Pitlochry road) and on the north by a line that runs along the A85 from Oban to Tyndrum, up the A82 to Rannoch Moor, then eastwards along Loch Rannoch and Loch Tummel to Pitlochry. In the south it is bounded by the central belt of Scotland between Glasgow and Edinburgh, below which the Southern Uplands continue to the English border.

The region itself is divided into two distinct halves by a geological zone of fracture known as the Highland Boundary Fault, which runs in a straight line across the breadth of Scotland from south-west to north-east. From the west coast it crosses Loch Lomond at Balmaha, passes through the Trossachs at Aberfoyle and heads north-east through Glen Artney to the Tay Valley and beyond, eventually to reach the east coast at Stonehaven.

Although the fault is hundreds of millions of years old, tremors are still felt along it as the rocks continue to settle, making the town of Crieff the earthquake capital of the British Isles.

South of the Highland Boundary Fault lie green rounded hills, while north of it lie rougher mountains, including all the region's 46 Munros and accompanying 21 Tops, to say nothing of 36 Corbetts. The rocks are mostly sedimentary but they have been greatly metamorphosed, uplifted and folded over time. Rolling folds parallel to the Highland Boundary Fault have rippled the land into Munro-height mountains separated by deep depressions, of which the largest is the great strath that runs from Crianlarich through Glen Dochart to Killin, then along Loch Tay to Aberfeldy and Pitlochry.

Although the ground to the north of the fault is rougher than that to the south, it is nowhere near as rugged as further north and west in the Highlands, while the igneous Cairngorm plateaus to the east are different again. The Southern Highland landscape is more gentle, more rounded and more verdant, though with enough geological variation and Ice Age sculpting to include an occasional rock playground for climbers and scramblers. Examples include the overhanging rock faces of The Cobbler, the great Prow of Stuc a' Chroin and the craggy corries of the Bridge of Orchy mountains.

Apart from some notable exceptions, the Munros cluster in groups separated by lochs and deep glens, which carry an extensive road system that eases access. Within each group the Munros are often close enough together to make multi-bagging trips practicable. The region therefore has the best of both worlds. Its Munros are easily accessible

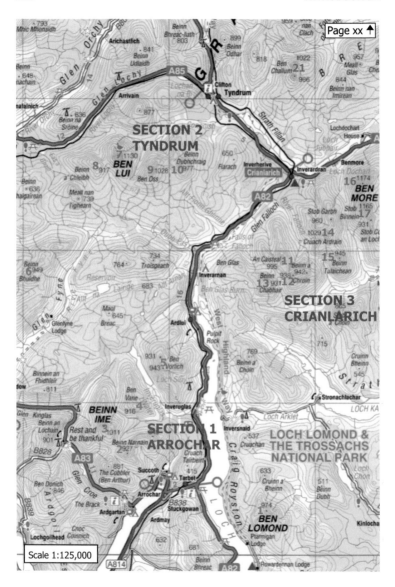

Route 1a Ben Lomond from Rowardennan: The Tourist Path

G1 ***** NS 360986, 8ml/12km, 1000m/3300ft

This route merits five stars if only for the ease and viewsomeness of the ascent, although some traditionalists may find the mountain today a tad too browbeaten for their tastes. The path begins inauspiciously behind the toilet block at Rowardennan car park, at the end of the road along the east side of Loch Lomond. Once you've found the toilet block, directions are superfluous. Just follow the person in front of you! Even if you find yourself in the newsworthy position of having the mountain to yourself, the path is unmistakable.

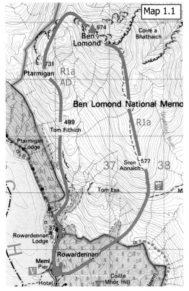

Map 1.1

It climbs through a forestry plantation onto open hillside and continues up grassy slopes to Sron Aonaich (*Strawn Ernich*, Nose of the Ridge, 577m/1893ft), where the angle eases at the start of Ben Lomond's broad south ridge. The summit looks disappointingly dull from here, like a great flattened pudding, but appearances are deceptive. The skyline is the lip of Coire a' Bhathaich (*Corra Vah-ich*, Corrie of the Byre), a craggy corrie hidden on the north side of the mountain (and whose name is misleadingly placed on the OS map).

The path rises gently up the south ridge before climbing more steeply to the corrie lip. The craggy corrie walls are too vegetated to offer much rock-climbing but, as they suddenly drop away beneath your feet, they certainly seem dramatic enough after the mountain's gentle southern slopes. The path continues along the corrie rim to the cliff-top ▲summit.

GiGi: For a novel approach, reach Rowardennan, on the east side of Loch Lomond, from Inverbeg, on the A82 along the west side. A ferry runs from Easter to October. It leaves Inverbeg at 10.30, 14.30 and 18.30, and Rowardennan at 10.00, 14.00 and 17.30. Enquiries: Rowardennan Hotel (tel: 01360-870273).

F-Stop: The isolated summit affords **tremendous views** in all directions, especially north into the Southern Highlands and south over Loch Lomond.

BEN LOMOND
Summit

Sron Aonaich

Torpedo: With judicious timing, Ben Lomond can be climbed between refreshment stops at one of east Loch Lomondside's numerous watering holes.

And if you're feeling energetic... the Ben Lomond Race record (up and down from Rowardennan Hotel) stands at just over one hour.

Needlepoint: Thanks to excellent paths, neither the Tourist Path up Ben Lomond's south ridge nor the Alternative Descent via Ptarmigan should cause problems in cloud.

Chilly Willy: Ben Lomond's popularity makes it a tempting winter objective but, when the Tourist Path is obliterated by snow, the mountain's steep upper slopes demand care. As always in winter, ice axe and crampons are *de rigueur*. In addition, beware cornices overhanging Coire a' Bhathaich. The Alternative Descent is a more serious winter proposition, owing to its steep start.

Summit

Coire a'
Bhathaich

Route 1a Alternative Descent:
Ben Lomond North-west Ridge and Ptarmigan

G3 ***** Add-on: negligible mileage, negligible ascent M3

To make a round trip that gives close-up views of Loch Lomond, we recommend a return over the subsidiary peak of Ptarmigan (731m/2398ft). The route is both more intricate and more fun than the Tourist Path, with an excellent path that has been less conspicuously renovated than the normal route. Be advised, though, that it is by no means the 'leisurely afternoon stroll' of the Tourist Path.

First you must descend Ben Lomond's steep north-west ridge. The stony path makes light of it, but there are two short rocky sections that require a spot of easy handwork. If you can manage the first, immediately below the summit, you should have no problems further down. Below the second rocky section, which is hidden from sight just below the first, the path winds its way invitingly down to and along Ptarmigan's undulating summit ridge.

After passing a hidden lochan, the **scenic descent** from the end of the ridge, with Loch Lomond and its mosaic of islands spread out before you, is the equal of any in the Highlands. The path reaches the lochside at a forest track that is part of the West Highland Way and which will take you back to Rowardennan.

Loch Lomond

Ptarmigan

Descending Ben
Lomond's NW Ridge

Tourist Path

Rowardennan

Loch
Lomond

Ptarmigan

▲**2 Beinn Narnain** 259 926m/3038ft (OS 56, NN 271066)
Meaning obscure. Perhaps Mountain of the Notches (*Ben Vyarnan*, from aspirated Gaelic *bearn*) or Mountain of the Alders (*Ben Yarnan*, from aspirated Gaelic *fearn*)

▲**3 Beinn Ime** 118 1011m/3316ft (OS 56, NN 255084)
Ben Eema, Butter Mountain (butter was once made at shielings in its corries)

The Cobbler   BEINN NARNAIN

Loch Long

Peak Fitness: No change since original 1891 Tables, although nearby Beinn an Lochain across the Rest and Be Thankful pass on the A83 was also a Munro from 1891 to 1981 (see Page 19 for further details).

Despite encircling roads, these Munros conceal their best features from roadside rubberneckers behind convex slopes, such that they are more interesting to climb than their initial inconsequential appearance would suggest. Beinn Narnain especially sports some sizeable summit crags that fringe **a plateau-in-the-sky summit**. The two mountains are separated by the 637m/2090ft Bealach a' Mhaim (*Byalach a Vaa-im*, Pass of the Moor), which can be approached from a number of starting points to

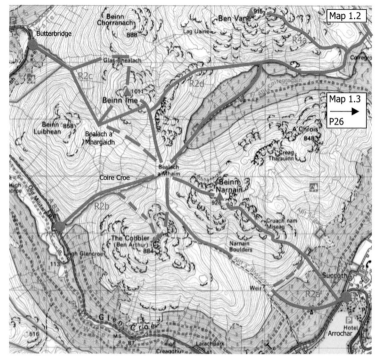

enable the two Munros to be bagged together by a variety of routes.

For a dual ascent, by far the most rewarding approach begins in the south-east near Arrochar (Route 2a). If you wish to avoid steep ground and the touch of rock, or are determined to set a new personal best, a shorter approach begins in Glen Croe to the south-west (Route 2b).

To climb Beinn Ime alone, an even shorter approach begins in Glen Kinglas to the north-west (Route 2c), while Beinn Narnain alone can be climbed by a truncated version of

Route 2a or 2b (although most will choose to extend the day to Beinn Ime). Note that Routes 2b and 2c, although shorter than Route 2a, ascend more tiresome terrain in duller country and in the event may seem not so short after all.

Ben Ime's main feature of interest is its rousing north-east ridge, situated at the heart of the Arrochar Alps and hidden from sight on most approaches. Intrepid scramblers may wish to consider it as **an adventurous wildside approach** to the two summits (Route 2d).

Route 2a Beinn Narnain and Beinn Ime
from Loch Long (Arrochar)

G3 **** NN 294049, 8ml/13km, 1300m/4250ft M8

When viewed from the shores of Loch Long, Beinn Ime is hidden behind Beinn Narnain, whose uninspiring lower slopes are overshadowed by the compelling rock faces of The Cobbler. But sulk ye not. Above the hillside in view, a broad, craggy ridge leads to Narnain's **scenic cliff-top summit**, with Beinn Ime readily accessible beyond.

The route begins just beyond the turn-off to Succoth on the A83 at the head of Loch Long, just outside Arrochar. Opposite the car park (small parking fee payable at machine), the new Cobbler Path begins a convoluted climb up the hillside, trending left into the glen of the Allt a' Bhalachain (*Owlt a Valachin*, Buttermilk Burn), between The Cobbler and Beinn Narnain. The path's first objective is the low point seen on the skyline at NN 280051, where the stream is dammed.

From the dam (marked as weir on OS map), a side path leaves the Cobbler Path to traverse right, back across the hillside, to the top of an old railtrack, where the Narnain path begins at a height of 330m/1100ft.

This point can be reached much

BEINN NARNAIN   The Spearhead

Summit

Cruach nam Miseag

The Spearhead

Spearhead Gully

Scramblers Route (see Page 13)

more quickly, and many would say much more enjoyably, by a direct ascent of the old railtrack. All that remains of the track, built during construction of the Loch Sloy hydro-electric scheme, is a line of intermittent concrete blocks, now linked by a rugged path. This path leaves the Cobbler Path c.70m from the roadside and climbs straight up the hillside. It is steep and rough but gains height fast and, unlike the Cobbler Path, makes you feel as though you're getting somewhere.

Above the railtrack, the Narnain path continues straight up the hillside. At first it is boggy in parts, it is indistinct in parts and it even crosses bare rock in parts, such that a spot of handwork may be required, but it improves with height and soon gives a straightforward ascent. At a height of

around 600m/2000ft it emerges onto Narnain's south-east ridge to open up views along Loch Lomond and over the Allt a' Bhalachain to the rock faces of The Cobbler.

As you continue up the ridge on grass among outcrops, one rocky knoll after another comes underfoot until you reach the 813m/2667ft highpoint of Cruach nam Miseag (*Croo-ach nam Mishak*, Mound of the Kid, i.e. Goat). A 30m/100ft dip then separates you from a final, steep, rocky 150m/500ft rise to Narnain's summit, and it is on this section that the real fun begins.

The gritty path calls for occasional handwork as it weaves a way up among the crags. At first it traverses to the left, quite exposed in places and a bit of a clamber in others, but fortunately never at the same time. Then it climbs back right to the foot of

Route 2b Beinn Narnain and Beinn Ime from Glen Croe
G1 ** NN 242060, 5ml/8km, 1160m/3800ft M8

If you need a couple of quick ticks on your list, an approach from Glen Croe gives the shortest round of the two Munros and, like an ascent via the Cobbler Path (see Page 12), offers a way up for those allergic to rock. However, it's a **criminally unscenic** way of reaching the summits. In fact, it's hard to believe the Arrochar Alps can look so dull.

While the Cobbler Path begins at sea-level on the south-east side of the Bealach a' Mhaim, the Glen Croe approach begins at a height of 170m/550ft on the south-west side, at the foot of Coire Croe (unnamed on OS map). There are parking spaces on the A83, beside the bridge over the stream that flows down the corrie, 5ml/8km outside Arrochar.

BEINN IME

NE Ridge

Bealach a' Mhargaidh

Bealach a' Mhaim

Coire Croe

BEINN NARNAIN

The start is confusing. White posts and a stile over a fence point the way up the right-hand (south) side of the stream, but the path there soon becomes boggy and indistinct.

Instead, go through the gate on the left and cross a bridge to find a better path up the left-hand (north) side of the stream. It climbs steeply up the hillside before easing off into grassy,

V-shaped Coire Croe, where you'll reach a small dam, half-way up to the bealach, at NN 252067.

Nondescript hillsides rise all around

BEINN IME

BEINN NARNAIN

Coire Croe

as the path continues to make its way up the corrie, eventually to become lost in thick grass as it nears the bealach. Once on the bealach, join Route 2a to knock off ▲Beinn Narnain and ▲Beinn Ime in turn.

NB If you wish to bag The Cobbler on the way back, you won't then have to retrace steps to the Bealach a' Mhaim as, from the summit, easy slopes descend directly north-west beside a stream to the dam in lower Coire Croe.

BEINN NARNAIN

Bealach a' Mhaim

BEINN IME

Needlepoint: Despite the featurelessness of the Bealach a' Mhaim, the Glen Croe approach gives more room for navigational error than Route 2a from Loch Long. On descent from the bealach in cloud, head south-west down the grassy hillside and you should meet the stream leading down to the roadside at some point.

Chilly Willy: Even when the mountains are snow-covered, this route lacks technical difficulty and is a more straightforward winter option than Route 2a. An ascent from Loch Long via the Cobbler Path and the Bealach a' Mhaim, as noted on Page 12, is equally easy and far more scenic, but twice as long.

there is some exposure towards the top, so we grade the route G4. Only you can decide whether such a prospect fills you with anticipation or dread.

To reach the ridge, follow Route 4a up Coiregrogain to the foot of Ben Vane, then continue along the Land Rover track until it reaches a small dam

The rocks begin... but which way up?

below a waterfall on a side stream (NN 279090). Here the track bears left into a forestry plantation and will form the return route.

On the far side of the dam, a rough path climbs steeply around rocks to reach the streamside above and follow it to the foot of the ridge, where the first **tiers of crags explode out of** **the moor**. We could tell you the best way up, but we're not going to, because that would spoil the fun. (If truth be told, we're not sure we know the best way up, but please don't rat on us.)

Above the first tiers is a small levelling then... well, there's more of the same. Unless you're as

Rock Tower

BEINN IME

Exposed Bypass path

Easier Bypass route

navigationally challenged as Needlepoint, you should experience no real problems until, beyond a small dip, you find yourself at the foot of a final rock tower. And an intimidatingly steep, exposed and vegetated beast of a thing it is too. You may well choose to sit here awhile and ponder.

Only the brave will tackle this **mother of all thrutches** direct, but the seemingly formidable upper rocks do have two lines of weakness – one in the centre and an easier one to the right.

Caution: Do not attempt a direct ascent of the rock tower unless you are a capable Grade 5 scrambler inured to exposure.

Fortunately there is an easier way to surmount the obstacle. Look for a small path that traverses left to climb around the tower and regain the ridge above. This path crosses very steep grass, is quite exposed and is not recommended to anyone too delicate to get their fingernails dirty, but it is much easier than a frontal assault. And there is a still easier option for those unconvinced of the adhesive properties of grass. From the dip before the tower, a developing path descends a hundred metres or so down stony slopes on the right, then climbs back around the side of the tower to regain the ridge.

Above the tower, the ridge levels and merges with Beinn Ime's southern hillside, where Route 2a is joined for the final spurt to the ▲summit.

Only after reaching the skyline seen above does the angle ease at last over a succession of levellings fronted by sizeable crags. The path threads a convoluted line around and over the rocks with several variations. Even on the easiest line you'll probably use hands in one or two places, but there's no exposure or danger. Other lines may require occasional thrutches that,

to the grateful amusement of companions, will be difficult to achieve with any semblance of dignity. A final rock step pops you out onto the small table-top ▲summit.

It is now apparent how the mountain derives its name, as it lies directly between Ben Vorlich and the rest of the Alps. Ben Lomond is also visible across Loch Lomond.

Needlepoint: In cloud you may never quite know where you are amid all the rock outcrops, but there are no subsidiary tops or ridges to mislead and the well-worn path should make the ascent fairly foul-weatherproof.

Chilly Willy: Ben Vane is no place to learn how to use ice axe and crampons. Under snow, the slopes of the south-east spur become intimidatingly steep and exposed, such that in some places a slip would be difficult to arrest.

GiGi: After rain an odd phenomenon occurs: a small lochan forms on Ben Vane's summit table-top.

Route 4a Alternative Descent: Loch Sloy
G2 *** Add-on: 1½ml/2km, zero ascent

If you are unfazed by pathless grass slopes that can be quite steep in places, this alternative descent route is well worth consideration. It avoids the retracing of steps down the south-west spur and passes a number of features of interest.

From Ben Vane's summit, stroll along the turf ridge that heads north-west around the skyline, aiming for the saddle below the subsidiary peak of Beinn Dubh (*Ben Doo*, Black Mountain). Before reaching the saddle, descend right into the **attractively**

BEN VORLICH

Loch Sloy

Rocky
Basin

BEN VANE

rugged, ice-scoured, lochan-filled basin between the two peaks.

This basin is so wide-open and complex that the way out of it is ridiculously difficult to spot. Aim left of the rocky highpoint seen on the lower basin lip to find a stream descending to Loch Sloy (N.B. *Not* the stream at the far right-hand side of the basin). As the stream tumbles down from the lip, a path on its left eases the initial

steepening and passes a jumble of giant boulders that harbour **a labyrinth of deep fissures** – well worth a careful look.

Below the boulders, yomp down the grassy hillside beside the stream until you can take an easy diagonal line down to Loch Sloy dam. Here you'll meet the paved road that will take you back down Coiregrogain to your starting point.

GiGi: The maze of fissures passed on the Alternative Descent is among a number of 'underground' features found around the Arrochar Alps. There are caves on The Brack, Beinn an Lochain and A' Chrois, numerous howffs such as the Narnain Boulders (see Route 2a), and more fissures high on the south-west side of Ben Vorlich above Loch Sloy dam.

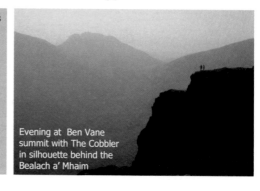

Evening at Ben Vane summit with The Cobbler in silhouette behind the Bealach a' Mhaim

▲6 Beinn Bhuidhe 216 948m/3110ft (OS 50 or 56, NN 203187) *Ben Voo-ya*, Yellow Mountain
(probably named for the subdued colouring of its vegetation)

BEINN BHUIDHE

Viewed from
Beinn Ime

Peak Fitness: No change since 1891 Tables.

The nondescript country to the north-west of Arrochar contains only one solitary Munro and is little visited. Even Beinn Bhuidhe itself, despite being the highest point, fails to stand out on the map. It fares little better on the ground. In fact, it is difficult to see at all behind the all-encompassing high moorland that surrounds it.

But don't let that fool you into thinking the mountain is easy pickings. The approach is tiring, the summit is guarded by crags, the ascent is steep, the route is vertiginous in places, the path crosses a number of rocky steps, routefinding is complex...

In short, Beinn Bhuidhe is **one awkward customer**.

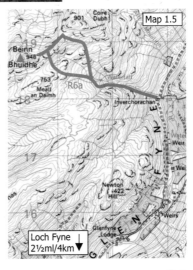

Map 1.5

Loch Fyne
2½ml/4km

Route 6a Beinn Bhuidhe from Glen Fyne

G3 *** NN 194125, 13ml/21km, 950m/3100ft M33

The route begins with a 4½ml/7km walk along Glen Fyne, most of it on a paved private road. There's a car park at the beginning of the road, just off the A83 at the head of Loch Fyne. The walk follows the river all the way, passing flat green fields between steep grassy hillsides. **Choose to enjoy it** - you won't be seeing Beinn Bhuidhe's retiring summit for some time yet.

After 3ml/5km, the paved road crosses the river to climb to a hidden reservoir. Leave it at this point to stay on the near (west) bank, where a Land Rover track continues to the locked bothy at Inverchorachan, at the foot of the mountain. At a gate just beyond the bothy, the climb to the summit begins on the near (south) bank of the Allt na Faing (*Owlt na Fank*, Stream of

the Sheep Fank or Enclosure).

A path climbs steeply beside the stream into a small gorge, where it becomes quite exposed on steep grass slopes. Above, a two-tiered waterfall tumbles from the skyline. Bhuidhe's summit, of course, remains well out of sight above there. The path negotiates a few rocky steps as it clings to the side of the gorge and, just before a levelling at the foot of the waterfall, **a granny stopper of a rock outcrop** may well give sensitive souls pause for thought. (NB It's not at all difficult.)

The path surmounts the waterfall by climbing diagonally left of it then cutting back right to the riverbank above, after which it leaves the Allt na Faing for good to veer left again into an ill-defined, knolly, confusing corrie. The path becomes indistinct but you

The Rock Outcrop

lowly Beinn a' Chleibh, little more than a flat-topped appendage on Lui's featureless western flanks, a readily baggable add-on.

There's no question, though, that as long as you don't suffer from vertigo, the longer eastern approach from Dalrigh gives a correspondingly more rewarding ascent (Route 7b). Beinn a' Chleibh is a more awkward add-on from this side, but you could always leave that for another day. Some mountains deserve to be seen at their best. Ben Lui is one of them.

Torpedo: Dalrigh is the starting point not only for the classic approach to Ben Lui but also for the ascent of the group's two other Munros - Ben Oss and Beinn Dubhchraig (Route 9a). Lui is separated from Oss by such an easy bealach that the three mountains could be climbed on the same trip (plus Chleibh?) to make a memorable round (see Route 9a Extension 1 on Page 60). Pardon? Of course you can.

BEN LUI

Stob Garbh

Coire an t-Sneachda

Coire Gaothach

Stob an Tighe Aird

Viewed from Ben Oss

GiGi: Tyndrum (*Tyne-drum*, from the Gaelic *Tigh an Druim*) means House on the Ridge. Dalrigh (*Dal-ree*, from the Gaelic *Dal Righ*) means King's Field. During his long campaign to impose himself as King of Scotland, Robert Bruce fought the MacDougalls of Lorn here in 1306. And lost.

He didn't get his own back until a rematch on the slopes of Ben Cruachan two years later. Lochan nan Arm (Lochan of the Weapon), on the south side of the River Cononish, derives its name from the legend that, during the retreat, Bruce threw his sword into it.

Route 7a Ben Lui and Beinn a' Chleibh from Glen Lochy (western approach: Fionn Choirein) NN 239278

Ben Lui and Beinn a' Chleibh: G2 *** 7ml/11km, 1100m/3600ft

Beinn a' Chleibh alone (for the pure of heart who have already climbed Ben Lui by Route 7b): G2 * 5ml/8km, 730m/2400ft

The western approach route offers the shortest way up Lui but manages to avoid completely all the best scenery. We give it a three-star rating for the summit environs, but only if you promise to **sit awhile at the cairn and meditate on why you came up this way**. However, unless you're allergic to the touch of rock beneath your fingers, you can go some way to redressing the balance of missing out on the east side of the mountain by taking a scrambly detour up the enjoyable north-west ridge (see Alternative Approach).

On their west sides, the summits of Ben Lui and Beinn a' Chleibh enclose the deep green bowl of Fionn Choirein (*Fyoon Chorran*, White Corrie). The corrie's main stream flows into another stream, confusingly named the Eas Daimh (*Aiss Daff*, Stag Waterfall), which eventually enters the River Lochy in Glen Lochy. Near the confluence with the Lochy, 6½ml/10km west of Tyndrum on the A85 road through the glen, the route begins at a Munro baggers' car park.

Both Munros rise stoutly out of the forest above the car park. Lui's north-

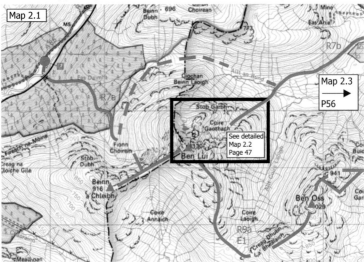

Option 1: North-west Arm Direct (G3). The north-west (right-hand) arm is regarded as the standard ascent route. The path up it is steep, stony and exposed, but it keeps you close to the scenery and requires no more than minor handwork.

Option 2: North-west Ridge via Coire an Lochain (G3). The north-west ridge lies over the right-hand skyline, beyond the north-west arm, on the far side of hidden Coire an Lochain. It is gentler and less exposed than the north-west arm, with a couple of easy rock steps to add interest.

Option 3: South-east Arm Direct (G4/G5). For expert scramblers in search of an adrenaline rush, the south-east (left-hand) arm gives a gravity-defying ascent up the narrow rock rib that separates Coire Gaothach from a hidden eastern corrie (Coire an t-Sneachda).

Option 4: South-east Ridge via Coire an t-Sneachda (G2). The easiest ascent route out of Coire Gaothach traverses left of the south-east arm to find an easy way up over the left-hand skyline via hidden Coire an t-Sneachda.

Which option to choose?

If you're in search of a testing scramble, consider going up the SE Arm Direct (Option 3) and down the NW Ridge (Option 2). If you enjoy a spot of handwork but nothing too demanding, and you don't mind a bit of exposure, go up the NW Arm Direct (Option 1) and down the NW Ridge (Option 2). If you want to avoid as much exposure and rockwork as possible, go up and down via Coire an t-Sneachda (Option 4), but take a look down the NW Arm (Option 1) and the NW Ridge (Option 2) and consider them as possible descent routes. To help you in your decision, we describe each option in detail.

Option 1: North-west Arm Direct (G3) M47

From the floor of Coire Gaothach, your first objective is the low point on the right-hand skyline, at the head of an open gully of grass and rocks behind Stob Garbh. There's a side path to the gully, but it is non-existent at first and therefore difficult to locate.

After reaching Coire Gaothach, the stream splits and, just above the confluence, the main path you've followed from the Allt an Rund crosses the main stream. At this crossing,

you've already missed the line of the side path to the gully 100m back. To find it, leave the main path at the stream crossing and climb the hillside on the right.

The side path makes a diagonal beeline for the top of the gully on grassy slopes to its right. Nearing the skyline, it no longer has any choice but to enter the steep, stony gully itself, but the going is neither exposed nor difficult and the skyline cairn is reached without much ado.

Once on the skyline, the view west opens up over the small lochan-floored Coire an Lochain to Lui's north-west ridge, with Ben Cruachan visible beyond. Above, the north-west arm rears up to the north-west top, promising **an adventurous finish to the ascent**. The path is steep, stony and occasionally exposed above big drops left into Coire Gaothach. With lots of rock around, there are one or two places where hands will prove useful. It's not difficult, but it requires care and concentration. The ridge tops out near the north-west top for a short walk to the ▲summit.

Note on descent: If you descend this way, the gritty path requires even more care than on ascent, and the fact that you'll be looking over the drops adds to the feeling of exposure. You may well discover backside holds you missed on the way up. If you don't fancy it, you'll have more fun going down the north-west ridge (Option 2) and crossing Coire an Lochain to regain the path at the low point on the skyline near the top of Stob Garbh.

Stob Garbh

Looking down The NW Arm

Option 2: North-west Ridge via Coire an Lochain (G3)
NN 265267, unnamed on OS 1:50,000 map M47

The north-west ridge lies across Coire an Lochain from the north-west arm. Compared to the latter, its angle is more gentle, there is less exposure and the path is more stable. A couple of rock steps require handwork, but they are easy, clean and non-exposed. Although technically harder than anything on the north-west arm, they are decidedly less unnerving than some sections of that route's gritty, exposed path. In fact they're fun.

After climbing from Coire Gaothach to the low point on the right-hand skyline, as described in Option 1, cross grassy Coire an Lochain with its tiny lochan to reach the upper north-west ridge (described as Route 7a Alternative Approach on Page 44).

Option 3: South-east Arm Direct (G4/G5) M47

The direct ascent of the south-east arm of Coire Gaothach gives **a pulse-pumping scramble** on the edge of the abyss. If you're an adrenaline junkie in search of excitement, as well as an experienced scrambler immune to exposure, this might be the one for you.

Caution: This is no place to practice rock skills. Expect loose rock, gritty stances and great exposure. As the ground is occasionally vegetated and the path loose, avoid when wet and manky (the route, not you).

SE Arm
upper section

Your first objective is the low point on the left-hand skyline, at the far left-hand corner of the corrie, at the very foot of the steep south-east arm. In the bowl of Coire Gaothach, the main path crosses the main stream and heads for that very spot. It soon becomes indistinct but, if you lose it, you'll pick it up again higher up. It climbs steep grass slopes left of a boulder ruckle to a short grass ramp, clearly seen from below, which cuts back left onto the low point of the skyline. You may choose to use hands for balance on the steep grass but it's not difficult.

Once on the skyline, the rocky south-east arm towers overhead. The ascent begins on a gritty path that climbs steeply to the foot of a nose of outcrops and vegetated ledges. The crest (G5) has the cleanest rock but is hard and very exposed above Coire Gaothach. The path (G4) manages to find an easier route to the left, away from the edge, but it too is exposed

Route 9a Ben Oss and Beinn Dubhchraig from Dalrigh

G3 ** Route Rage Alert NN 344291, 10½ml/17km, 1170m/3850ft M56
(*** if you have a helicopter to bypass the approach wallow)

Begin at Dalrigh car park (as for Route 7b). Steps at the far end of the car park descend to a road that leads to a bridge over the River Cononish. On the far side of the bridge, turn immediately right on a Land Rover track that leads to a bridge over the West Highland Railway line at NN 336285.

On the far side of the railway bridge, a boggy path branches right to a footbridge over the Allt Gleann Auchreoch at NN 333284. You can avoid the boggy going by continuing up the track to a left-hand bend, from where drier paths lead back down to the footbridge. On the other hand, you might as well accustom yourself to the boggy stuff now.

On the far side of the footbridge, a path goes up the right-hand side of the Allt Gleann Auchreoch and then the right-hand side of the Allt Coire Dubhchraig, climbing all the way through Coire Dubhchraig to two lochans on Beinn Dubhchraig's summit ridge. We trust your boots are waterproof and advise you to **pack a snorkel**. If you want to detour around the worst of the bog, check out the Alternative Approach.

The sodden path passes through the **beautiful old pine forest** of Coille Coire Chuilc (*Cull-ya Corra Cool-ak*,

BEINN DUBHCHRAIG

NE Ridge

NW Ridge

two lochans

N Ridge

Coire Dubhchraig

Viewed from near Dalrigh

Wood of the Reedy Corrie), although, conditions underfoot being as they are, you may find its beautiful oldness hard to appreciate. You may find it even harder to understand how Dubhchraig acquired its imposing name (the 'black crag' is on the south side of the mountain).

The underfoot morass deteriorates still further as you leave the wood and climb through newer forestry plantations. When the trees finally begin to thin out at their upper boundary, don't let quagmires draw you away from the streamside path as it makes its way into the vast open spaces of shallow Coire Dubhchraig.

Here at last matters start to improve. The stream itself forms **an attractive series of cascades** as it drops over a long staircase of ledges. The path remains boggy in parts but

feels like baked earth compared to what you've just negotiated.

Should you have made it this far, there is a choice of ways out of the corrie. Dubhchraig's summit is on the left, at the head of the north-east ridge, but the path follows the stream right to climb diagonally across the corrie to two skyline lochans at the junction of north and north-west ridges. The path has one steep section beside a waterfall before it peters out near the lochans, from where an indistinct path continues up the broad north-west ridge to the summit.

The shorter north-east ridge, which starts steeply but eases with height, carries no more than traces of path but is equally easy and has better views and better going on grass and boulders. In addition, by ascending this way, you won't have to retrace

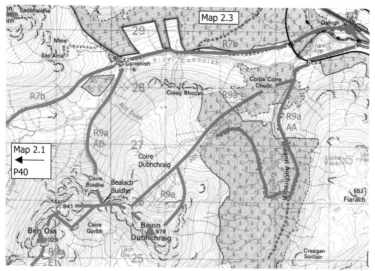

to the ▲summit (see Route 11a for details). Beyond the summit, instead of continuing down the main path to the An Caisteal bealach, bear left around the rim of Coire a' Chroin to its western point, called Carn Liath (*Carn Lee-a*, Grey Cairn). From here, descend south-east down crag-free slopes to regain the Land Rover track back to the road.

Needlepoint: In cloud, the featureless southern flanks of Beinn a' Chroin do *not* make for ideal hillwalking. On ascent, crags loom out of the mist to complicate routefinding, while on descent you'll have to trust the compass/GPS.

Chilly Willy: In winter be prepared to encounter very steep, very tiring snow slopes with varying degrees of exposure. The best line should cause no major problems for those competent on such terrain, but you may not find the best line.

Baffies recommends a heatwave diversion: Just above the Land Rover track, the Ishag Burn forms some picturesque pools and waterslides that, on a hot summer's day, it would be criminal not to sample.

Route 11d Beinn Chabhair alone
from Beinglas Farm (Glen Falloch)
G2 *** NN 321187, 7ml/11km, 940m/3100ft M67

Map note: The whole route is on both OS 50 and OS 56.

As Beinn Chabhair is separated from its two neighbours by an awkward bealach, it is usually climbed on its own from Beinglas farm, 6ml/10km south of Crianlarich on the A82. This approach doesn't show the mountain to advantage, as it forsakes picturesqueness of scenery for ease of ascent, but those in search of more adventurous fare will find a variation that compensates for this deficiency (see Alternative Descent). Parking is permitted at Beinglas farm but, if the car park is full, you can park at

Inverarnan (NN 319188), an old drovers' inn on the A82 300m south of the farm access track.

If starting at Inverarnan, follow the farm access track over the bridge across the River Falloch, then turn immediately right on a signposted path that leads to the West Highland Way, right of the farm buildings. The farm car park is in front of the buildings. Behind the wooden 'wigwams' to the right of the buildings, follow the Way over a stile in a wall, then take the obvious path that zigzags up the hillside through sparse woodland left of the Ben Glas Burn.

A steep climb brings you to Ben Glas Falls, a series of cascades where the burn tumbles 36m/120ft down the '**Devil's Staircase**'. The path tends to channel water after rain, but of course that's the best time to visit the spot. Above the falls, the path emerges into a wide-open upper glen and continues along the streambank to

Lochan Beinn Chabhair at the foot of its namesake peak. The path is a quagmire in places, but overall it gives a pleasant enough streamside ramble through 'undemanding' scenery to the reedy lochan.

The nondescript summit of Beinn Chabhair now rises ahead, sporting an infinite variety of ascent routes on grassy slopes among crags. For the most straightforward way up, look to the left, where a boulder slope rises to a notch on the north-west ridge, between Meall nan Tarmachan (no, not the Meall nan Tarmachan of Section 6) and Beinn Chabhair.

A developing path starts up the line of the stream that descends from the notch, then grassy slopes climb right to gain the ridge itself. Once on the ridge, the path becomes well-defined and easy to follow as it twists its way upwards around outcrops. After reaching a subsidiary top, the ▲summit is only a short stroll away.

notch

BEINN CHABHAIR

Lochan Beinn Chabhair

Lochan a' Chaisteal

Beinn Chabhair NW Ridge

Needlepoint: The development of a Munro baggers' path has made a once problematic route now easy to follow in cloud, but the Alternative Descent down the complex north-west ridge remains a navigational nightmare.

Chilly Willy: There are no especial difficulties in winter, although you are likely to encounter steep snow in several places on the ascent from Lochan Beinn Chabhair to the summit.

If snow is low on the hill, or the ground is icy, the steep drops above Ben Glas Falls can become exposed and dangerous. In such conditions, it is safer to use the Alternative Start.

Route 11d Alternative (Gentle) Start NN 326202 M67

About 1½ml/2km north of Beinglas farm, the A82 briefly crosses the River Falloch and a farm track leaves the roadside to give an alternative access point to the western slopes of Beinn Chabhair. Keep left at a fork and, at a prominent tree only a couple of hundred metres from the roadside, fork left again on an ATV track (marked as a path on the OS map). The track climbs the hillside and joins the path from Beinglas farm at the 300m contour (NN 329182), well above Ben Glas Falls, at the entrance to the upper glen.

The disadvantages of the Alternative Start are the addition of 1ml/1½km to the round trip and the bypassing of the waterfall. The advantages are a much less steep, much less exposed and much less boggy approach path.

Route 11d Alternative Descent:
Beinn Chabhair North-west Ridge

G2 **** Extra mileage: negligible; Extra ascent: negligible;
Extra effort: considerable M67

Left of the skyline notch above Lochan Beinn Chabhair, the north-west ridge is a confusing **maze of knolls and unexpected drops**. For anyone still suffering from a surfeit of energy at the summit of Beinn Chabhair, the descent of the ridge makes an adventurous return route past the **secret beauty spot** of Lochan a' Chaisteal. This handsome lochan is encircled by castle-like crags (hence its name), which give it a rare air of seclusion high above the surrounding glens.

Stob Creag an Fhithich

AN CAISTEAL

BEINN A' CHROIN

BEINN CHABHAIR

Lochan a' Chaisteal

Needlepoint: To be avoided in mist.

Baffies: To be avoided, full stop.

On descent from the summit of Beinn Chabhair, leave the path on approach to the notch and stay on the ridge. Go over Meall nan Tarmachan, descend steeper slopes to a dip on its far side and cross another rise. Ahead now is craggy Stob Creag an Fhithich (*Stop Craik an Ee-ich*, Peak of the Raven's Crag), which can be bypassed on the left to reach Lochan a' Chaisteal.

The lochan marks the end of the ridge but not the end of the adventure, as the hillside beyond, which separates you from the ascent path, is beset with yet more knolls and crags. With judicious routefinding you should be able to find a way down (let's hope so, anyway).

To avoid very steep ground above the Bein Glas Burn on the left (south) side of the ridge, keep heading west until you can see a way down. To this end, although it may seem counter-productive at first, begin by keeping the highpoint of Meall Mor nan Eag (*Myowl Moar nan Aik*, Big Hill of the Notch) to your left. It would be a good idea to recce the terrain on the outward trip.

Route 16a Ben More and Stob Binnein from Benmore Farm: Benmore Glen

G2 **** NN 414258
Ben More alone: 6ml/10km, 1000m/3300ft
Add-on Stob Binnein: 1ml/1½km, 300m/1000ft

Two routes up Ben More begin at Benmore farm, on the A85 2ml/3km east of Crianlarich. Route 16b is shorter but relentlessly steep. Route 16a described here takes a more roundabout but considerably less arduous approach, making it the easiest route on the mountain.

From roadside parking just east of Benmore farm, a signposted path joins a Land Rover track up Benmore Glen beneath Ben More's grassy western slopes. When the track ends, a somewhat boggy path continues up beside the Benmore Burn.

Your first goal is the 862m/2828ft Bealach-eadar-dha Beinn, the aptly named bealach between Ben More and Stob Binnein (*Byalach-aitar-gha Ben*, literally the Bealach-between-two-mountains).

It is tempting to take a diagonal short cut up the grassy hillside to reach the bealach but, if you yield to temptation, you'll find yourself on increasingly steep, pathless terrain. The best line holds to the glen as far as the stream prior to the one that comes down from the bealach. There's a large boulder just before this stream

BEN MORE   STOB BINNEIN
S Ridge
Benmore Glen   Bealach-eadar-dha Beinn
Stob Garbh
Inverlochlarig Glen

joins the Benmore Burn at NN 421235. A developing path goes up the stream's right-hand side, crosses to the bealach stream and climbs the right-hand side of that past numerous small waterfalls and pools that tempt on a hot day.

Once on the bealach, Ben More's broad south ridge rears overhead, giving a steep but easy 312m/1024ft climb to the ▲summit. A few rock obstacles on the gentle summit slopes are easily bypassed, but you may have more fun going over them.

After returning to the bealach, the 303m/994ft return trip up and down Stob Binnein's stony north ridge, rimming broken crags at the head of Coire Chaorach, is less steep. The zigzagging path soon deposits you on the **appealingly castellated** ▲summit.

STOB BINNEIN

BEN MORE

Needlepoint: Use the streams that flow down from the Bealach-eadar-dha Beinn as a guide and you shouldn't go far wrong on ascent in cloud.

Chilly Willy: Owing to their height and central location between the east and west coasts of Scotland, Ben More and Stob Binnein attract more snow than most other Southern Highland peaks. The slopes that rise to the two summits on either side of the Bealach-eadar-dha Beinn can become appreciably steep swathes of snow and ice in winter. Stob Binnein's north ridge especially becomes **a beautifully corniced 300m sweep of snow** that is a joy to crampon. It was a winter visit here in the 1870s that made Bill Naismith (of Naismith Rule fame) realise that the Scottish mountains deserved as much respect as the Swiss Alps.

Route 16b Ben More and Stob Binnein from Benmore Farm: Ben More North-west Spur

G3 **** NN 414258 M86
Ben More alone: 4ml/6km, 1000m/3300ft
Return via Benmore Glen: add-on 1ml/1½km
Add-on Stob Binnein: 1ml/1½km, 300m/1000ft

Ben More's north-west spur is the mountain's traditional ascent route, but it is nowhere near as carefree a jaunt as might be expected of such an accolade. It takes **a directissima line** up the steep grass slopes above Benmore farm, left of a shallow corrie, rising 1000m/3300ft in only 2ml/3km. Sure, it's the shortest way up, and it's certainly less boggy than the Benmore Glen route (Route 16a), but increasing exposure with height may daunt the nervous, while you can be assured that **the word relentless was coined to describe the ascent**. Fortunately the extensive northern view, expanding panoramically with height, can be regularly invoked as an excuse for rest stops.

Beginning as for Route 16a, follow the Benmore Glen Land Rover track as far as a gate in a fence near the foot of the spur. Twenty-five metres beyond the gate, the climb begins on an indistinct path that heads up the hillside. Don't worry if you lose it, as the lower slopes can be climbed anywhere. Higher up, aim right to gain the rim of the shallow corrie, where the now well-worn path becomes increasingly welcome as the ground steepens even more. Given such terrain, the corrie's Gaelic name

BEN MORE

NW
Spur

seems entirely apposite: Sloc Curraidh (*Slochk Coory*, Difficult Pit).

At the head of the corrie the path climbs beside an old dyke through very steep rocky ground. It is barely necessary to put hand to rock, but anyone who is nervous of heights will *not* be enamoured either of the gritty

path or the steep drops into the corrie, which is why we grade the route G3. Above the rocks, gentler slopes continue to the ▲summit. Whether you continue to ▲Stob Binnein or not, the Benmore Glen route via the Bealach-eadar-dha Beinn (Route 16a) gives a more pleasant return journey.

STOB BINNEIN

BEN MORE

Needlepoint: The steep ground beside and above the Sloc Curraidh demands care in cloud. On ascent make sure you find the path up the left-hand rim to avoid straying onto difficult terrain.

If descending this way, it is even more imperative to come off Ben More's featureless summit slopes in the right direction and find the path. Take note on the way up or return via the much easier Benmore Glen route.

Chilly Willy: Avoid this route in winter. A slip above the Sloc Curraidh could prove fatal and has done so in the past. The very steep slopes of the upper NW Spur are in any case prone to avalanche.

For a safer (though still steep) approach to the summits in winter, with ice axe and crampons of course, ascend via Benmore Glen (Route 16a) or Stob Binnein's South Ridge (Route 16d).

Baffies: Enjoy! I'll wait for you in the Benmore Restaurant on the outskirts of Crianlarich.

Route 16c Ben More and Stob Binnein from
Coire Chaorach: Ben More North-east Ridge

G2 (optional G3) ***** NN 455276 M86
Ben More alone: 7ml/11km, 1010m/3300ft
Add-on Stob Binnein:
    return via Ben More:
        2ml/3km, 620m/2050ft
    return via Bealach-eadar-dha Beinn and Coire Chaorach:
        2ml/3km, 300m/1000ft
    return via Stob Coire an Lochain and Coire Chaorach:
        2ml/3km, 450m/1500ft

An ascent of Ben More's north-east ridge is the most **exciting and aesthetically satisfying** route to the summit of the mountain, although it makes reaching Stob Binnein a lengthier endeavour. Two steepenings, neither of which need be difficult, add zest to proceedings. More aggravating is the problem of reaching the ridge in the first place, courtesy of afforestation around its foot, but the directions given here should enable you to surmount the forest without undue hassle.

Just west of the bridge over the Allt Coire Chaorach, 5ml/8km east of Crianlarich, a forest road leaves the A85 to run up Coire Chaorach on the east side of Ben More. It is proposed to build a car park near the start of the road, but at the time of writing the route begins at a lay-by 100m west of the bridge, from where a path leads to the road.

Follow the road to a junction at a hairpin bend, stay left on the main road and follow it up Coire Chaorach for around another 1500m. Twenty-

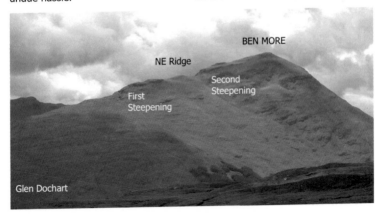

BEN MORE

NE Ridge

Second
Steepening

First
Steepening

Glen Dochart

BEN MORE

Second
Steepening

Bypass
Path

Top of First Steepening   NE Ridge

five metres beyond a vehicle turning point, a cairn marks the start of a rougher track that climbs to the upper forest boundary.

Note that this cairn can also be reached by a second, grassier track. This leaves the forest road at NN 451272, just around the first left-hand bend after leaving the car park, and takes a lower-level route through the forest. Some may find its woodland meanderings more pleasant than the forest road, and it should certainly be used to avoid vehicle traffic during forestry operations.

After quitting the forest road at the cairn just beyond the vehicle turning point, the rougher track crosses the stream coming down from Coire Clach (*Corra Clach*, Stony Corrie – the shallow corrie on the south-east side of the north-east ridge) and exits the forest at NN 458255. About 100m

after crossing the stream, at a small clearing on a left-hand bend, you can take an easy short-cut up through the remaining trees. Once out onto open ground, bear right to climb the grassy hillside to the crest of the north-east ridge. NB At the time of writing it is proposed to construct a path through the forest beside the Allt Coire Clach to shorten the approach route.

You arrive at the foot of the good stuff, known as Sron nan Forsairean (*Strawn nan Forseran*, Nose of the Foresters), when the ridge narrows and rears up more steeply and rockily. A path picks an easy but entertaining route up the crest of the first steepening, then an agreeable stroll across a short level section brings you to the foot of the second, rockier steepening. Scramble up or take the easy bypass path on the right to reach broken ground that rises more gently

To find the bypass path from the bealach, contour around the foot of the rocks into the little corrie. The path is easy to follow for a while but becomes increasingly indistinct until, in the bowl of the corrie, it becomes lost in rock debris from storms of 2004. You'll find it again as it climbs out of the head of the corrie to the low point on the skyline of the north-west ridge. The ascent is problem-free, but steep and rough enough in places for those who eschew the use of trekking poles to use hands for balance.

The path tops out at a large cairn on the corrie rim, where it joins another path up the Prow's easy north-west ridge. At the foot of the final boulder slope, a smaller cairn marks the spot where a path goes diagonally right to Stuc a' Chroin's summit, some 500m metres to the south across gently rising ground. Alternatively, continue to the top of the Prow for a view of Ben Vorlich over the crags, then cross the broad connecting ridge to the Stuc's ▲summit.

To re-descend to Ardvorlich, first return to the Bealach an Dubh Choirein, taking as much care on descent as on ascent. On the left (west) side of the bealach you'll find a

Torpedo: If omitting Stuc a' Chroin, the simplest way back to Ardvorlich from Ben Vorlich's summit is to reverse the ascent route. For variety, you could return via the Bealach an Dubh Choirein and Coire Buidhe, as described in the main text, but there's another tempting alternative if you fancy a longer day out, although it involves rougher going.

Descend Vorlich's grassy south-east ridge to the wilds of Dubh Choirein (see Route 18d for description), then return northwards to Glen Vorlich through **an inviting rocky defile** on the east side of the mountain. The path through the defile, although still marked on most maps, has succumbed to the ravages of time and now gives boggy going for much of the way.

Choose to enjoy the experience thus: if you have generosity of spirit to spare, embrace the ecological development as an example of nature reclaiming its own, otherwise welcome it as a crowd deterrent. Not until it reaches the 500m/1650ft mark in Glen Vorlich does the 'path' develop into the grassy track that rejoins the outward Land Rover track at NN 630218, as noted on Page 99.

BEN VORLICH E top

... in winter

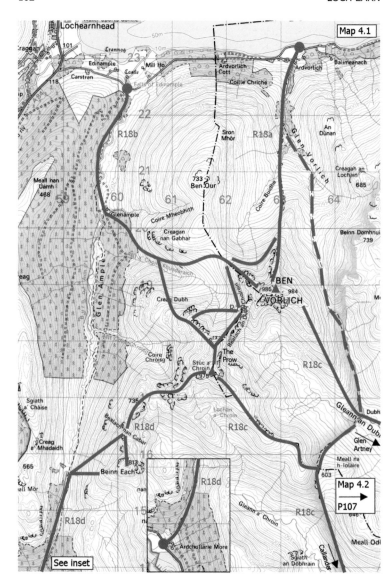

Map 4.1

Map 4.2
P107

See inset

path that contours around the upper reaches of Coire Fuadarach to a saddle on Ben Vorlich's north-west ridge, at the head of Coire Buidhe. The path is indistinct and boggy for a while but improves as it approaches the ridge. From the saddle, it contours around the right-hand side of Coire Buidhe to rejoin the ascent route at the start of the renovated path (as noted above).

STUC A' CHROIN

The Prow

SE Ridge

NW Ridge

Bypass path

Bealach an Dubh Choirein

BEN VORLICH SW Ridge

Needlepoint: The renovated path up Ben Vorlich rivals the Ben Lomond Tourist Path as the easiest foul-weather ascent in the Southern Highlands. Finding your way up and down Stuc a' Chroin in cloud is a different creel of herring.

When approached from Vorlich via the Bealach an Dubh Choirein, with rock looming out of the mist everywhere, the variety of route options can be confusing. On ascent, take care not to be led onto difficult ground. This is true even on the Prow bypass path, which is difficult to follow in places owing to rock debris.

The Stuc's summit cairn is perched at the cliff edge overlooking Gleann an Dubh Choirein. Don't confuse it with a larger cairn set back c.70m from the cliff edge (see Route 18d).

On descent, if using the Prow bypass path, take care to descend from the right spot, from the large cairn on the north-west ridge, not the smaller one higher up. For an easier route in cloud, use Route 18c.

Chilly Willy: Ben Vorlich is a popular winter goal from Lochearnside but **its convex upper slopes are deceptively dangerous** when iced. Near the summit, on the rim of the north-east corrie, a slip would be difficult to arrest, even with an ice axe, and that makes the standard ascent route from Ardvorlich a more awkward proposition than many expect. Accidents have happened here.

When approached from Ben Vorlich, *all* routes up Stuc a' Chroin, including the Prow bypass path, become snow and ice climbs in winter.

Route 18b Ben Vorlich and Stuc a' Chroin
from Glen Ample

Ben Vorlich + Stuc a' Chroin: NN 602224 M102
    G3 (with G4/G5 options) **** 9½m/15km, 1110m/3650ft
Ben Vorlich alone via its NW Ridge: G2 *** 7ml/11km, 890m/2900ft
Stuc a' Chroin alone via its NW Ridge: G2 ** 8ml/13km, 880m/2850ft

Map note: As for Route 18a, OS 51 is required in addition to OS 57.

This route vies with Route 18a as the easiest approach to a round of the two Munros, courtesy of an ATV track that climbs to a height of c.600m/2000ft on the flanks of Ben Vorlich's north-west ridge, in the upper reaches of Coire Fuadarach. The Bealach an Dubh Choirein is at the head of the corrie, with Stuc a' Chroin's Prow in view all the way up.

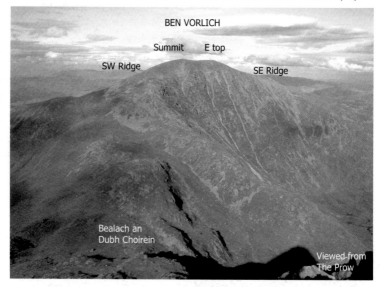

BEN VORLICH

Summit   E top

SW Ridge   SE Ridge

Bealach an
Dubh Choirein

Viewed from
The Prow

From the **picturesque Falls of Edinample** on the South Lochearnside road, take the Land Rover track up Glen Ample to Glenample farm. The footbridge over the Burn of Ample at NN 596203, opposite the farm, was washed away by a flash flood in August 2004, so follow these directions carefully:

After the track bridges the river at

NN 596208, leave it for a path that runs along the riverbank around the farm perimeter fence. This leads to another track beyond the farm buildings. Go right along this track to a stream less than 100m away. On the stream's far (right-hand) bank, a short path climbs to another track. Cross this second track (ignore any signposts that direct you along it) and continue up beside a fence for less than 100m to a reach a third track.

This is the track you want. Improving with height, it climbs through forestry plantations onto open hillside, eventually becoming a grassy ATV track that climbs high into Coire Fuadarach. It gives a painless approach walk, easily the equal of that from Ardvorlich, and it has the additional benefit of providing ever more imposing views of the looming Prow of Stuc a' Chroin.

When the track ends, gentle grass slopes climb to a saddle on Vorlich's north-west ridge, where you'll cross Route 18a return path from the Bealach an Dubh Choirein to Coire Buidhe. If you're lucky, you'll find an occasional path to ease the ascent. The ridge steepens near the skyline, where it joins the upper south-west ridge for the last short stretch to Ben Vorlich's ▲summit.

Continue to ▲Stuc a' Chroin as per Route 18a, then return to the Bealach an Dubh Choirein and descend across upper Coire Fuadarach to rejoin the approach track. If you'd prefer to avoid the environs of the Prow on descent, descend the Stuc's north-west ridge until you have outflanked all crags (including the rock buttress at NN 613186), then descend easier slopes into Coire Fuadarach. Note that, summer or winter, this line offers the easiest route up and down Stuc a' Chroin from Lochearnside.

Needlepoint: Although the approach track doesn't go all the way to Ben Vorlich's summit, keep heading upwards from its end and you should get there even in cloud. Foul-weather considerations for Stuc a' Chroin are as for Route 18a.

Chilly Willy: For a winter ascent of Ben Vorlich, the Coire Fuadarach approach avoids the problem of Route 18a's deceptively steep finish. Depending on the precise line taken up the north-west ridge, however, you may still encounter pockets of steep snow. Winter considerations for the connection to Stuc a' Chroin are as for Route 18a.

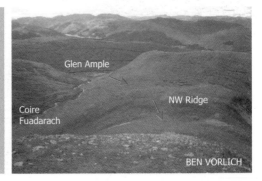

Glen Ample

NW Ridge

Coire Fuadarach

BEN VORLICH

Route 18c Ben Vorlich and/or Stuc a' Chroin from the South-east: Callander

Ben Vorlich + Stuc a' Chroin: NN 636107 M102/107
    G3 (with G4/G5 options) *** 13ml/21km, 1250m/4100ft
Ben Vorlich alone via its SE Ridge: G1 *** 13ml/21km, 1170m/3850ft
Stuc a' Chroin alone via its SE Ridge: G1 *** 12ml/19km, 810m/2650ft

O n their south-east sides, far from the Lochearnside trade routes to the north, both Ben Vorlich and Stuc a' Chroin throw out long, gentle, grassy ridges that would receive more attention were they easier to reach. If you're looking for an individual ascent of either mountain that avoids the steep sections of Routes 18a and 18b, both ridges give excellent walking.

However, unless you're perverse by nature, the approach to the foot of the ridges may seem less than excellent, which is why we can't bring ourselves to award these south-east routes more

than three stars. Long miles of remote, screamingly featureless back-country terrain are not everyone's cup of cranachan.

We suspect few will be tempted this way for a first ascent of the two peaks, but for a second ascent... or if you wish to avoid summer weekend crowds... or if you hanker after a walk on the wild side...

The shorter of two possible approaches begins at the end of the minor road past Bracklinn Falls north of Callander. There are parking spaces at the end of the public road, where a

STUC A' CHROIN

SE Ridge

From Callander

branch forks left to Drumardoch farm. A second approach begins at the end of the public road in Glen Artney

further east, although this one really is for masochists only (Route 18c Alternative Approach).

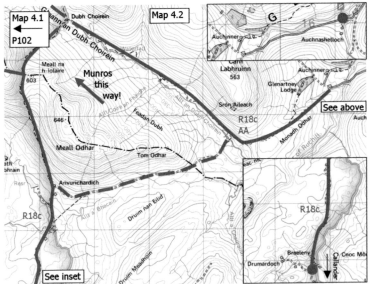

From the road-end near Drumardoch on the Callander approach, follow the continuing Land Rover track past Braeleny farm to the boarded-up buildings at Arivurichardich (try saying that fast). This is **unashamedly dismal country**, with undulating terrain dented by glens so broad and shallow they barely merit the name.

Just below Arivurichardich the track crosses the Keltie Water, whose bridge was washed away by storms in 2004. On a good day you can use stepping stones to cross both the river and a tributary just upstream of the former bridge. At other times you may need

to paddle. And remember there are yet other times when the water is high enough to wash away a bridge.

From the left-hand side of the upper building at Arivurichardich, the route continues on a former stalkers' path that has seen better days but still gives reasonably good going (except after rain). After a couple of hundred metres, at a fence, it forks. Take the right branch to climb diagonally up the hillside onto the south-east ridge of Stuc a' Chroin, eventually reaching the skyline near the small hump of Meall na h-Iolaire (*Myowl na Hillyera*, Hill of the Eagle).

If heading for Stuc a' Chroin, follow

the continuing path up the inviting ridge (see description below). For Ben Vorlich, cross to the far side of the ridge and descend a frustrating 150m/500ft to the ruined shieling of Dubh Choirein at the foot of Vorlich's south-east ridge. The path marked on most maps has been much reclaimed by the moor, making for somewhat boggy going, but it's not far down.

Dubh Choirein is perhaps **the most forlorn and lonely spot in the Southern Highlands**. It so well deserves its Gaelic name (meaning Black Corries) that on a dreich day it is a relief to leave it behind before you succumb to existential despair about the inequities of life.

BEN VORLICH

Bealach an Dubh Choirein

SE Ridge

Gleann an Dubh Choirein

Viewed from Stuc a' Chroin SE Ridge

Heading skywards once more, clingy moor and peat hags are soon happily left behind for the grassy south-east ridge and a nice wee path that makes for **a surprisingly diverting ascent**. Approaching Vorlich's east top, a rocky steepening looks like it might quicken the pulse, but the path weaves its way up easily onto gentle slopes above. The east top is soon reached, followed by the ▲summit. If continuing to Stuc a' Chroin, see Route 18a.

From the ▲summit of Stuc a'

Chroin, descend that mountain's south-east ridge to rejoin the outward route near Meall na h-Iolaire. The broad ridge, which revels in the quixotic name of Aonach Gaineamhach (*Ernach Ganavach*, Ridge of Fine Sand), gives a perfect evening stravaig down a couple of miles of **beguiling greensward**. Approaching Meall na h-Iolaire, you may be concerned that the path is descending further right than expected. Don't worry – it won't let you down.

Route 18c Alternative Approach from the South-east: Glen Artney

Ben Vorlich and Stuc a' Chroin: NN 711161 M102/107
G3 with G4/G5 options ** 14ml/22km, 1080m/3550ft
Ben Vorlich alone via its SE Ridge: G1 ** 12ml/19km, 830m/2750ft
Stuc a' Chroin alone via its SE ridge: G1 ** 14ml/22km, 820m/2700ft

All routes: + 2ml/3km road walk (1ml/1½km each way)
All routes: ** (more if you have a need to be alone)

Only those who revel in contrariness need bother to read this. The Glen Artney alternative approach to Route 18c involves more road walking, worse going and even duller scenery. The glen's one claim to fame is that it lies on the Highland Boundary Fault, which separates two distinct geological periods.

The sandstone hills to the south are in the Lowlands, while the mica schist hills to the north (including the two Munros) are in the Highlands. Not that knowledge of these facts is likely to ameliorate one's verdict on the dreariness of the scenery.

Beginning at the car park 1ml/1½km from the road-end, walk to the road-end then bear left on a Land Rover track that crosses a low moor to a junction in Gleann an Dubh Choirein. The track is good as far as here, but it deteriorates to a tiresomely boggy path as it continues along the

riverbank up the view-free glen to the ruins at Dubh Choirein.

Climb Ben Vorlich and/or Stuc a' Chroin as described opposite. If climbing the Stuc and descending its south-east ridge to Meall na h-Iolaire, you can avoid the boggy re-descent to Dubh Choirein. Instead, take the stalkers' path down to Arivurichardich and the rutted Land Rover track that runs from there back to the track junction in Gleann an Dubh Choirein.

STUC A' CHROIN

The Prow

SE Ridge

Needlepoint: In cloud, the south-east ridges of both Ben Vorlich and Stuc a' Chroin remain pretty straightforward, but the dismal countryside is even more depressing than in fine weather. Considerations for the crossing of the Bealach an Dubh Choirein to link the mountains are as for Route 18a.

Chilly Willy: Under normal winter conditions, both south-east ridges remain straightforward, although the rocky steepening on Vorlich's south-east ridge may give sport if the path is obliterated by snow. Considerations for the crossing of the Bealach an Dubh Choirein to link the mountains are as for Route 18a.

Route 18d Stuc a' Chroin alone from Loch Lubnaig: South-west Ridge

G2 ** (more if you're an awkward bagger) Route Rage Alert
NN 583136, 7ml/11km, 980m/3200ft M102

This is the shortest way up Stuc a' Chroin, but it's **a pernickety little route** whose quirky character will keep you on your toes all the way. For non-scramblers who don't wish to bag Vorlich as well, it offers a way up that completely avoids the Prow, but it is nowhere near as easy an ascent route as Route 18c. Although its **'enigma variations'** can prove diverting if you're in the mood, it is definitely not an option for someone simply seeking a straightforward saunter to the summit.

Point 735

STUC A' CHROIN

Viewed from
Beinn Each

The ascent begins well enough, on the signposted 'public footpath to Loch Earn via Glen Ample,' which leaves the A84 at Ardchullarie More on the shores of Loch Lubnaig (car parking in layby). A couple of hundred feet up, ignore a minor right branch and follow the main path left over a small stream to climb steadily through deep forest and join a forest track.

The angle eases as the track exits the forest and traverses the hillside to the long, flat saddle leading over to Glen Ample. The track itself becomes very boggy, but a path to its right finds drier going.

The hill on the right is Beinn Each (*Ben Yech*, Horse Mountain). Your first objective is the Bealach nan Cabar (*Byalach nan Cabbar*, Antler Pass), which separates Beinn Each from Stuc a' Chroin further along.

5 GLEN LOCHAY

At the west end of Loch Tay, Glen Lochay curves deep into the hills north of the Tyndrum/Crianlarich/Killin road through Strath Fillan and Glen Dochart to give access to six flanking Munros. Unfortunately, although the glen itself is picturesque enough, in a green, serene and undemanding kind of way, the featureless hillsides that rise to the heights are rather less inspiring, especially when cloud hangs low on the hill.

When viewed from the glen, only Ben Challum at its head is shapely enough to catch the eye, but it stands so far beyond the end of the public road that it is usually climbed via its less attractive south side above Tyndrum (Routes 21a and 21b). Creag Mhor, on the other hand, turns out to be more interesting than its lower slopes suggest (Routes 24a and 24b).

The remaining four Munros are, to be kind, **unrepentant heaps**. Meall Ghaordaidh's south-east ridge at least gives a straight up and down route (Route 26a), but Meall Ghlas and Sgiath Chuil (Routes 22a, 22b and 22c) and Beinn Heasgarnich (Route 24c) could sprawl for Scotland.

CREAG MHOR

BEINN HEASGARNICH

Glen Lochay

▲21 Ben Challum 106 1025m/3363ft (OS 50, NN 386322)
Calum's Mountain, possibly named for St. Columba
△South Top 998m/3275ft (OS 50, NN 342420)

Peak Fitness: No change since 1891 Tables.

At the head of Glen Lochay, Ben Challum's domed summit tops a craggy north face whose bounding north-west ridge beckons ascent. Another high-level ridge, slung between summit and South Top, promises more good times.

You just knew there'd be a catch, didn't you? Here it comes: from the end of the public road in Glen Lochay there's a 6ml/10km walk-in, eventually pathless, to the Bealach Ghlas Leathaid (*Byalach Glass Lyeh-at*, Pass of the Green Slope) at the foot of the north-west ridge. You'd have to be made of stern stuff to opt for that over the much shorter approach from the A82 Tyndrum road on the south side of the mountain.

Challum itself is well aware of such modern hillwalking sensibilities and, in a fit of pique at those who shun the northern profile it would prefer to present to the world, hides its summit from the Tyndrum road behind a terminally dreary southern hillside.

The **tiresome trade route** up the mountain wends its weary way up this hillside, morphing bright-eyed baggers into crestfallen footsloggers (Route 21a). Those who have never felt the lure of hillwalking wonder what we more enlightened souls see in it. The view of Challum's lower slopes from near Tyndrum may well make you wonder yourself.

But there's good news for those who prefer something a tad less soporific. For the sake of an extra couple of miles, and to get yourself into Challum's good books, you can approach the north-west ridge from the Tyndrum side. We wouldn't recommend this route to anyone seeking an easy life but, if you can handle a spot of steep, off-path terrain, never was a bit more effort so richly rewarded (Route 21b).

BEN CHALLUM   S Top

NW Ridge

Gleann a' Chlachain

F-Stop: The summit panorama goes some way to compensate for the dull ascent by the normal route. The mountain's isolation gives it good all-round vistas of Southern Highland Munros, especially the near-at-hand Crianlarich and Tyndrum groups.

GiGi: St. Fillan, one of the prime movers in Scotland's uptake of Christianity, came to Strath Fillan from Iona around 664 and established a monastery at what is now Kirkton farm. For centuries the sanctuary was a haven of peace and learning in troubled times. In the fourteenth century Robert Bruce upgraded it to a priory, which it remained until falling into disrepair after the seventeenth century Reformation.

Route 21a Ben Challum from Kirkton Farm (near Tyndrum): Southern Slopes

G1 ** Route Rage Alert NN 355282, 7ml/11km, 900m/2950ft

Challum's summit environs deserve more than two stars, but the traditional ascent route probably deserves less. From the lay-by on the A82 opposite Kirkton farm, 2ml/3km east of Tyndrum, take the farm access road across the River Fillan (bridge) to join the West Highland Way.

Follow the Way to the farm buildings and the ruins of St. Fillan's priory (see Page 119). Immediately beyond the ruins, when the Way turns left, keep straight on along a farm track that leads up to and across the West Highland Railway line.

About 50m beyond the railway crossing, quit the track to climb diagonally right to a deer fence that can be seen above. Beside the fence you'll find a path that goes all the way to the summit. The fence veers much further right than seems warrantable, but the path hasn't developed here for no reason. Stick with it.

The main interest on ascent lies in avoiding the numerous sections of marshy ground. About half-way up, when the path temporarily levels off

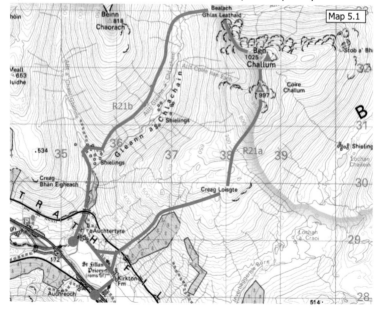

Map 5.1

atop Creag Loisgte (*Craik Loshka*, possibly Burning Crag, from Gaelic *Loisg*), there's one stretch of bog that is particularly amusing.

Beyond here, with the unremarkable skyline of the South Top in view at last, the path continues its ascent on the right of the now broken fence. The angle steepens, but improved going more than compensates, courtesy of a stony path that climbs slopes of short grass and boulders.

Matters become more interesting at the ΔSouth Top, and about time too, where a curious little defile separates the cairned highpoint from the continuing ridge to Ben Challum's main summit. The ridge is quite narrow and rocky at first, though of zero difficulty. It soon becomes grassy again, giving **an agreeable high-level stroll** as it broadens across a shallow bealach to reach steeper, rockier slopes that climb to the ▲summit.

BEN CHALLUM

NW Ridge

S Top

Needlepoint: The complex topography of the South Top makes it a very confusing place in cloud. On descent, after leaving the cairn on the highest point (and make sure you *are* on the highest point), it is important to find and keep to the path beside the fence. The fence doesn't reach all the way to the top but cairns lead down to it. If you can't see these, aim due south until you do.

The north-west ridge provides a more well-defined route to the summit in cloud, but an optimal line through the rock outcrops will be less easy to find.

Chilly Willy: Under snow, the ridge connecting South Top to summit gives the kind of **silly-grin-making ridge walk** for which the Scottish mountains were designed. In some conditions, though more rarely than in former years, a narrow snow arête forms. There is normally no undue difficulty for anyone properly equipped, but take care at the summit, which is perched close to cornices that form on both north and east sides.

The north-west ridge gives a more difficult winter ascent on steep snow slopes beside the rock outcrops.

Route 21b Ben Challum from Auchtertyre Farm (near Tyndrum): North-west Ridge

G2 (with G3/G4 options) **** NN 354290, 9ml/14km, 900m/2950ft M120

A southern approach to Ben Challum's **entertaining north-west ridge** is made practicable by a Land Rover track that climbs Gleann a' Chlachain (Glen of the Village) on the mountain's west side. There are many places where the presence of such tracks detracts from the hillwalking experience. This isn't one of them.

The route begins at Auchtertyre farm at the foot of the glen. A Land Rover track, part of the West Highland Way, connects the farm to Kirkton farm about ½ml/1km away. You could begin on the Kirkton farm access road, as per Route 21a, but at the time of

writing you can drive up to Auchtertyre farm and begin there.

Park in the car park just before the bridge that leads to the farm and take the continuing Land Rover track that runs up the left-hand side of Gleann a' Chlachain. Keep right at a first fork then left at a second to follow the track high up the glen between Beinn Chaorach (*Ben Cheurach*, Sheep Mountain) and Ben Challum.

When the gravelly surface turns to grass, contour across tussocky ground at the head of the glen to reach the Bealach Ghlas Leathaid at the foot of Challum's north-west ridge.

BEN CHALLUM

The Castle

NW Ridge

Route 22c Sgiath Chuil alone
from Auchlyne (Glen Dochart)

G2 ** NN 447275, 9ml/14km, 780m/2550 M126

This Glen Dochart approach can't avoid the rough going of Route 22b altogether but, as a way of climbing Sgiath Chuil alone, it provides an easier ascent route than that from Auchessan. Admittedly it is 2ml/3km further, but 5ml/8km of it is on a Land Rover hydro track.

Sgiath Chrom   SGIATH CHUIL   Meall a' Churain

Glen Dochart

The track begins on the east side of the West Water at Auchlyne, reached by a minor road from the A85. Park at or near the start of the track with care and consideration. The track zigzags up to a fork, branches left and undulates across the hillside towards Sgiath Chuil, seen ahead. To avoid rough ground, stay on the track as far as a small dam on a side stream at NN 480303 (the track continues to the larger dam on the Allt Coire nam Moine, noted opposite).

From the small dam, climb straight up the hillside of thick grass above, staying right of the craggy southern slopes of Sgiath Chrom (*Skee-a Chrome*, Curved Wing). On improved going, bear left along the top of the crags, following the ridge line over or around Sgiath Chrom's highpoint, to the broad saddle below the summit of Sgiath Chuil. The ▲summit crags are easily breached by the gap to their left (south-west).

SGIATH CHUIL

▲**24 Creag Mhor** 84 1047m/3434ft (OS 50, NN 391361)
Craik Voar, Big Crag
△Stob nan Clach 956m/3137ft (OS 50, NN 387351)
Stop nan Clach, Stony Peak
▲**25 Beinn Heasgarnich** 62 1078m/3536ft (OS 51, NN 413383)
Ben Heskarnich, Sheltering Mountain (from Gaelic *Seasgairneach*)

Stob nan Clach

Sron nan Eun

CREAG MHOR

Glen Lochay

Peak Fitness: No change to Munros/Top since original 1891 Tables. Stob an Fhir-Bhoghe (*Stop an Heer Voa-ha*, Archers' Peak) was also a Top until 1981.

As is often the case in Glen Lochay, these Munros are characterised by **long, grassy slopes that climb endlessly skywards**. Unusually, rock outcrops dot the hillsides, which you'd think might make for a more interesting ascent than usual hereabouts. In truth, alas, the lasting memory you'll have of these mountains is of slogging up steep grass slopes *around* the crags. Never will you have been more grateful for a high starting point.

Now for some good news. Like Ben Challum, which it faces across upper Glen Lochay, Creag Mhor is a good-looking mountain when viewed from the upper glen beyond the road-end,

BEINN HEASGARNICH

Stob an
Fhir Bhoghe

Kenknock

Sron
Tairbh

Bealach na
Baintighearna

Viewed from
Creag Mhor

even if its aspiring name flatters to deceive. Its **attractively pointy summit** stands at the head of the deep hole of Coire-cheathaich (*Corra Chay-ich*, Misty Corrie), whose skyline gives **a scenic horseshoe ridge walk** that is the best day out in the glen (Route 24b). Ascent to and descent from either end of the horseshoe is steep but, once up, that only adds to the high-level ambience.

Creag Mhor is separated from its neighbour Beinn Heasgarnich by the deep, 650m/2150ft Bealach na Baintighearna (*Byalach na Ben-tyurn-a*, The Lady's Pass). It is a long way down and an even longer way up again to Heasgarnich's summit but, as it adds negligible extra mileage to the return trip from Creag Mhor,

most people grit their teeth and go for it (Route 24a). Unfortunately, Heasgarnich makes a wearisome anticlimax and, even worse, you have to forsake half of Creag Mhor's horseshoe ridge in order to bag it.

So therein lies the rub... Do you climb Creag Mhor as it was designed to be climbed, via the horseshoe, and leave Peskynich for another day (Route 24c), or do you bag the two in a oner? Of course, you could always leave the decision until you reach the summit of Creag Mhor.

Knowing you as we do, we suspect you'll probably return over Peskynich, but just for that we'll subtract one star from the route's rating for failing to complete the otherwise four-star Creag Mhor horseshoe.

Route 24a Creag Mhor and Beinn Heasgarnich from Glen Lochay

G2 *** NN 461370, 12ml/19km, 1170m/3850ft M136

Map note: As the mountains are on separate maps, the route requires both OS 50 and OS 51.

From the end of the public road along Glen Lyon, just beyond Kenknock farm, a hydro maintenance road climbs north up the hillside to cross into Glen Lyon. Through access to Glen Lyon may or may not be possible for private transport, but you can drive to a hairpin bend less than a mile up. The route begins here, at a high starting point of 350m/1150ft, on a Land Rover track that heads west

into upper Glen Lochay across the lower slopes of Beinn Heasgarnich.

Leave the track at the Allt Batavaim after 3ml/5km to climb the steep, grassy hillside of Sron nan Eun (*Strawn nan Yai-un*, The Bird's Nose) – the end point on Coire-cheathaich's north-east rim. Bands of crags complicate the ascent. You can climb around them to the left or, for more sport, pick a route up grassy rakes

CREAG MHOR

SE Ridge

Sron nan Eun

▲**29 Meall Corranaich** 68 1069m/3507ft (OS 51, NN 615410)
Myowl Corranich, possible meanings include Hill of the Lament (from Gaelic *Corranach*), Hill of the Bracken Corrie (from Gaelic *Coire Raineach*) and Sickle-shaped Hill (from Gaelic *Corran*)

▲**30 Meall a' Choire Leith** 261 926m/3038ft (OS 51, NN 612439) *Myowl a Chorra Lay*, Hill of the Grey Corrie

MEALL CORRANAICH

Coire Gorm

MEALL A' CHOIRE LEITH

Peak Fitness: No change to Munros since original 1891 Tables. Sron Dha Mhurchaich, an insignificant rise on Meall Corranaich's south-west ridge, 800m from the summit at NN 615410, was an additional Top from 1891 to 1921.

These two rounded summits to the north-west of Beinn Ghlas complete the trio of Munros west of Ben Lawers. Overshadowed in bulk by Lawers to the east and in ruggedness by Meall nan Tarmachan to the west, they are the highpoints on a gentle grassy ridge that runs north-south beside the Lochan na Lairige road.

The most practicable and popular way of bagging the pair begins at the road's highpoint, 3ml/5km north of the Visitor Centre. From here the two summits are equidistant, making a circular trip possible (Route 29a). Unfortunately, boggy approaches make for a 'mixed' hillwalking experience, definitely not one for which the Lawers Range would prefer to be remembered. A more interesting approach to Meall Corranaich begins on its south side at the Visitor Centre, but it makes Meall a' Choire Leith more awkward to reach (Route 29b).

Route 29a Meall Corranaich and Meall a' Choire Leith from Lochan na Lairige road highpoint

G2 * Route Rage Alert NN 593416, 6ml/10km, 730m/2400ft M148

From the cairn at the highpoint of the Lochan na Lairige road, 3ml/5km beyond the Visitor Centre, the ridge that curves south-eastwards to the summit of Meall Corranaich is an obvious approach route. From the parking space below the cairn, walk back along the road, around the right-angled bend, to find the start of the path just before the first passing place. Don't confuse this path with the return path, which leaves the road 20m earlier, at the corner.

The path is boggy in its lower reaches, but the route to the ▲summit is straightforward, with **zero features of interest** to warrant description.

The going improves higher up, when the south-east ridge joins the more well-defined south-west ridge for the final part of the ascent.

Continuing northwards to Meall a' Choire Leith, a good path on short turf gives **an amiable stroll** down a broad, gentle ridge. This is much more like it. After a short rise, the ridge broadens even more and divides around Coire Gorm (*Corra Gorram*, Blue Corrie). The lie of the land tempts you left onto the corrie's left-hand rim (the north-west ridge). Instead, keep right to follow the north ridge around the right-hand rim and up to the flat ▲summit of Meall a' Choire Leith.

MEALL A' CHOIRE LEITH

MEALL CORRANAICH

To return to your starting point, descend Meall a' Choire Leith's steep, grassy south-west slopes into Coire Gorm and tramp up the boggy upper reaches of Gleann Da-Eig. A swampy path takes the best line, crossing the Allt Gleann Da-Eig at a small dam, but in many places it is more of a hindrance than a help.

Cross the low bealach south of the hillock called Meall nan Eun (*Myowl nan Ee-an*, Hill of the Birds) to regain the roadside. As a parting shot by which to remember the two Munros, the peat hags on the bealach will act as a litmus test of your capacity to maintain a humorous disposition in the most dire of circumstances.

stream coming down from Meall Greigh, climb its left-hand side. Higher up, trend right onto the skyline to find a path leading to the pudding-shaped ▲summit.

Heading west to Meall Garbh, a gentle knobbly ridge descends to the intervening 834m/2736ft bealach, known as the Lairig Innein (*Lahrik Inyan*, Anvil Pass, unnamed on OS map). Steeper grass slopes then climb to Meall Garbh's north-west shoulder, where the angle of ascent eases as the ridge veers south-west around the head of the eastern corrie.

A couple of hundred metres before the summit, you'll pass a curious transverse ridge, whose cairned high-point can mislead in cloud. At the ▲summit itself, the view west opens up and affords a first opportunity to study in detail the redoubtable north-east face of An Stuc. Unless continuing to it, return to the bealach below Meall

Greigh and scamper down to the dam on the Lawers Burn. If you wish to visit nearby Lochan nan Cat, a path of sorts (boggy after rain) follows the south bank of the burn from the dam to the lochan's mouth.

On the map, it may seem tempting to descend from Meall Garbh to the An Stuc bealach and from there to the head of the lochan beside a tumbling stream, but we wouldn't recommend it. The hillside below the bealach consists of very steep, wet grass among sizeable crags. It's *possible* to make a way down left of the stream, but it's not pleasant. Acolytes of

> **GiGi**: The Lawers Burn cuts a curiously deep trench into the hillside, with raised banks that are additionally notable for their innumerable ruined shielings, especially at East Mealour (NN 676415). These are a poignant reminder of the days when Lawers village was the populous centre of a flax spinning industry.

MEALL GARBH

Grassy hill No. 2   MEALL GREIGH

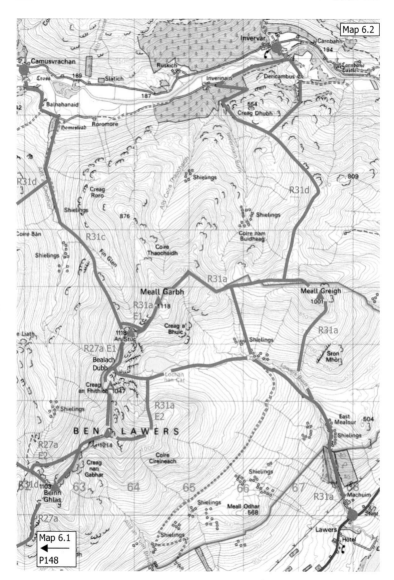

Map 6.2

Map 6.1
←
P148

Route 31b An Stuc alone from Lawers Village (Loch Tay)

G3 *** NN 680400, 9ml/15km, 940m/3100ft M160

Anyone wishing to avoid the adrenaline rush of the north-east face or the long haul from Ben Lawers, can bag An Stuc on a separate expedition using either of two easy approaches. A southern approach from Lawers village (described here) is more scenic but, if you've been up the Lawers Burn path already, to bag Meall Greigh and Meall Garbh, you might wish to consider a northern approach from Glen Lyon, which is both wilder and even easier (Route 31c).

From Lawers village, follow the Lawers Burn path to its end at the dam, then continue along a boggier path left of the stream and around the southern shore of Lochan nan Cat. Above the lochan, the stream that descends from the Bealach Dubh left of An Stuc tumbles down a gully.

Climb the steep grass slopes left of the stream. There is no path at the time of writing, but this may change in time. As lines of attack merge, traces of path are already appearing.

On steeper ground higher up, those who eschew trekking poles may find hands useful for balance. The easiest line veers left, away from the stream, to enter a small upper corrie. At the back left-hand corner of the corrie, a path right of the stream climbs a small defile to gain the skyline at the low point of the bealach.

The climb from there up the south-west side of An Stuc, as previously noted on Page 163, is steep but straightforward. You may use hands for balance at one rocky spot, but there's an unmistakable path all the way to the ▲summit.

Torpedo: A continuation over Ben Lawers, up the north ridge and down the east ridge (described opposite as Route 31a Extension 2), is an attractive option for a longer day. Add-on: 1ml/2km, 280m/900ft.

Needlepoint: In cloud, a crag-free line between Lochan nan Cat and the Bealach Dubh can prove surprisingly difficult to find, especially on descent.

Chilly Willy: Although straightforward in summer, this route can become unexpectedly difficult in winter. Be prepared for very steep snow below the Bealach Dubh and on the south-west ridge of An Stuc, which can seem quite exposed when the path is iced or snow-bound.

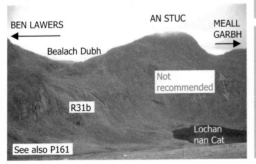

BEN LAWERS   AN STUC   MEALL GARBH

Bealach Dubh

Not recommended

R31b

Lochan nan Cat

See also P161

Route 31c An Stuc alone from Camusvrachan (Glen Lyon): North Ridge

G2 *** NN 620477, 8ml/13km, 940m/3100ft M160

If you wish to avoid the steep south side of An Stuc above Loch Tay, the north ridge gives a satisfyingly straightforward approach that is both the easiest way up and the least known. It is *so* little known that the ridge carries no path as yet, but the terrain is excellent and the route has an attractive air of wildness on the 'backside' of the Lawers Range.

On the south side of the Glen Lyon road near Camusvrachan house, a side road leads down to a bridge over the River Lyon. There are parking spaces just before the bridge, on whose far side the road is for private use only. Walk up the road to a T-junction, then go left along a Land Rover track for around ½ml/1km to the bridge over the Allt a' Chobhair (*Owlt a Ko-ur,*

Foaming Stream).

On the far side of the bridge, a gate on the right gives access to a grassy track up the glen of the Allt a' Chobhair. It climbs through a defile into the level basin of a hidden upper glen, at whose back the Munros of the Lawers range burst into view one by one. The track runs pleasantly beside the stream, passes some ruined

visit both west top and ▲summit, you could go up one way and down the other. Both are easy.

If only the same could be said for the purgatorial re-descent of the Coire an Dothaidh path, which lurks in wait at the end of the day to enable the swear box to be filled to overflowing.

W top   BEINN AN DOTHAIDH
                              Summit   SE top

Needlepoint: The well-worn path up Dorain makes the ascent virtually foul-weatherproof, but beware the false summit, which has fooled many a mist-enshrouded walker over the years, especially in days of yore before the path became so distinct. How many Munroists believe they've climbed the mountain but haven't? And did the unknown Sassenach believe he was at the summit when he built his cairn here?

Dothaidh is a bigger foul-weather challenge. The tilted summit plateau of moss and grass is notoriously difficult to navigate in mist. As well as the west top and summit, there is a lower south-east top to add to the confusion.

When trying to find the summit, the rim of the north-east corrie is a useful navigation aid, but don't get too attached to the convex corrie edge or you may end up taking a closer look at the crags than intended. On descent, if you don't find and keep to one of the paths, the Dorain–Dothaidh bealach may be harder to locate than anticipated.

F-Stop: The summits of Dorain and Dothaidh both give wide-ranging views westwards to the Glen Etive hills and the Blackmount. The best viewpoint of all, however, is Dothaidh's west top, which boasts an **immense panorama** over Rannoch Moor to the Nevis Range.

Chilly Willy: In winter, Coire an Dothaidh becomes a snow bowl whose steep flanking hillsides are prone to avalanche. It is no place for beginners but, in good condition, makes an enjoyable winter training playground for those moving on to more difficult winter ascents. Although the route to the bealach has no technical difficulty, steep snow will be encountered on ascent to the upper corrie.

Above the bealach, climbing Dorain and Dothaidh is no more difficult than reaching the bealach in the first place. At Dothaidh's summit, beware cornices overhanging the north-east corrie rim. As a winter bonus, the boggy approach path to Coire an Dothaidh is easier to negotiate when the ground is hard.

Route 35b Beinn Dorain alone from Auch Farm: South Ridge Direct

G3 *** NN 317354, 6ml/10km, 910m/3000ft M182

This route up Dorain isn't readily combined with an ascent of Dothaidh to the north as it goes straight up Dorain's **skyrocketing south ridge**, which rises 850m/2800ft in 1ml/1½km. The very sight of it from the A82 north of Tyndrum is going to make you wish you were fitter.

The route up is fairly problem-free, but to say that it is one long, steep, challenging, relentless, pathless ascent is an understatement. It has a sting in the tail and is no route for those who suffer from vertigo or want an easy life, yet we have a sneaking admiration for its refusal to kowtow to accepted standards of angularity and give it three stars for sheer effrontery.

BEINN DORAIN

S Ridge

Auch Gleann

The bottom section of the ridge forms a craggy nose that is best avoided on the right. To outflank it, begin at Auch farm access road, as per Route 39a, and follow the Auch Gleann Land Rover track to the railway viaduct. Once under the viaduct, ford the Allt Kinglass and climb the steep slope in front of you to a shoulder above the rocks.

Having reached the south ridge proper, the angle of ascent lessens, though not enough to make any appreciable difference to the effort required. At least there are views west now into the Central Highlands. Lying in wait up ahead, meanwhile, to keep your mind occupied, is that sting in the tail...

Just below the summit, a rock band extends across the whole width of the ridge and seems to block the way. It can in fact be outflanked on steep grass slopes to the right (which probably make the best descent route), but there is a fascinating alternative solution to the problem.

If you head straight up the centre of the rock band, on an apron of grass that leads right into the crags, you'll find a hidden grassy gully that curves up left to the top of them. It's a hands-and-feet clamber, but it's not difficult. The ▲summit lies not far above.

No sweat.

Looking down the route through the rock band

The rock band

Needlepoint: In cloud, just keep heading skywards and you should reach the summit, but take careful note of the route through the rock band for the return trip.

Chilly Willy: Very steep, very exposed snow slopes understandably make the south ridge route a rarely attempted winter venture.

Baffies: Food for thought: *Dorainn* (NB with a double 'n') is a Gaelic word meaning Pain or Torment. If the person who named the mountain first climbed it by the south ridge…

Route 35c Beinn an Dothaidh alone
from Achallader farm: North-east Ridge
G2 *** NN 322443, 6½ml/11km, 840m/2750ft M182

This round trip on the north side of Beinn an Dothaidh isn't readily combined with an ascent of Dorain to the south, but it could be combined with ascents of Beinn Achaladair and Beinn Chreachain (see Route 37a Extension 1). As a route to Dothaidh's summit, its advantage over Route 35a is that it ascends and descends around the rim of the north-east corrie (up the north-east ridge and down the south-east ridge), giving **close-up views of impressive rock scenery** from the two shapeliest ridges on the mountain.

NE Ridge

NE Corrie

BEINN AN DOTHAIDH

The north-east corrie is an off-shoot of Coire Achaladair, which lies between Beinn an Dothaidh and Beinn Achaladair. Beginning at Achallader farm, take the Coire Achaladair path as far as the corrie entrance (see Route 37a for details), then cross rising moor to gain the right-hand rim of the north-east corrie.

The going is rough at first, but ground vegetation soon diminishes to give a less fraught approach than you might anticipate when you first step off the path.

On initial steep slopes that rise to a shoulder, take a curving line to the right to outflank outlying crags and emerge at a levelling overlooking the

the Hillocks), the track goes straight on beside a tributary (the Allt a' Chuirn). There are three more fords to come, but by now the stream is usually shallow enough to be crossed on stepping stones.

The track forks at the foot of Beinn a' Chuirn. Follow the right-hand branch to its end on the bealach leading to Loch Lyon, where weirs and waterslides on the Allt a' Chuirn may prove irresistible on a hot day. As an excuse for a lengthy sojourn, you can use the time to study the unfamiliar

backsides of Beinn Dorain and Beinn an Dothaidh before tackling the toughest part of the day – a 480m/1550ft ascent on steep grass up Coire a' Chuirn (unnamed on OS map) to the Mhanach–Chuirn saddle above.

The Allt a' Chuirn comes down from the saddle and indicates the line to be taken. The hillside can be climbed on either side of it. On the right-hand side, you can veer away to head directly for Mhanach's summit. More congenially, stay on the left-hand side, where a very rough track gives you a

LAWERS RANGE

Loch Lyon

View from Beinn Mhanach

F-Stop: Beinn Mhanach's summit view, in all directions, seems to be **too finely tuned for coincidence**. To the west, the four higher Bridge of Orchy Munros are close at hand, but who would expect Ben Nevis to be *just* visible over the Achaladair–Chreachain bealach, or Ben Alder to be *just* visible across Rannoch Moor around the flanks of Chreachain? Walk to the east end of the summit plateau and you'll find an even more stunning view, along Loch Lyon to Ben Lawers.

head start, the cooling stream stays close at hand on a hot day, and the angle eases off towards the saddle. Above the saddle, gentle turf slopes climb to the flat, stony ▲summit.

Before descending, you may wish to make the short trip across the intervening saddle to bag △Beinn a' Chuirn, whose summit requires an ascent of only 74m/243ft.

Needlepoint: Navigation should remain straightforward, even in cloud.

Chilly Willy: A good, steep snow plod, but a long walk-in on a short winter's day.

Route 39a Alternative Descent from Beinn a' Chuirn
G2 * Add-on: 1ml/1½km M182

Whereas the right-hand branch of the Auch Gleann track ends at a height of 370m/1200ft on the bealach leading to Loch Lyon, the longer left-hand branch ends at a height of 550m/1800ft beneath the craggy western front of Beinn a' Chuirn. The additional height makes this a tempting ascent alternative, but that craggy hillside has to be outflanked further along, in the vicinity

of the Achaladair–Chuirn bealach, where marshy going will make you wish you'd gone the other way.

If you nevertheless decide to descend this way from Beinn a' Chuirn to make a round trip, stay well right on leaving the summit, aiming in the direction of Beinn a' Chreachain, until you can see easy grass slopes curving back left to the Achaladair–Chuirn bealach (see also next route).

BEINN MHANACH

BEINN HEASGARNICH

Beinn a' Chuirn

BEINN ACHALADAIR

Loch Lyon

Coire Daingean

bealach

Viewed from Beinn an Dothaidh

Route 39b Beinn Mhanach from Achallader Farm via Dothaidh–Achaladair bealach G1 *

Return trip from bealach: 5ml/8km, 430m/1400ft M182
+ Return trip from Achallader farm to bealach: 10ml/16km, 1010m/3300ft

On the plus side, this route up Mhanach is slightly shorter than Route 39a and involves a less steep final climb. On the minus side, there is more ascent and worse terrain. In practice, as the route goes over the Dothaidh–Achaladair bealach, you'd only use it for an add-on bagging trip to Mhanach while making other ascents in the area – Beinn an Dothaidh (Route 35c) or Beinn Achaladair + Beinn a' Chreachain (Route 37a Extension 2). For strong walkers it is perhaps the most popular route up Mhanach, but we give it one star only for the summit view.

From the Dothaidh–Achaladair bealach, reached from Achallader farm by Route 37a, make a descending traverse of Achaladair's grassy eastern hillside to the 638m/2093ft Achaladair–Chuirn bealach. The key to an effortless traverse is a narrow path that connects the two bealachs. From the cairn on the Dothaidh–Achaladair bealach, at the top of Coire Daingean, look for another cairn, 70m away across the bealach, that marks the start of this traverse path.

It is not a great path, but it improves after a wet start and does the business before disappearing on the marshy Achaladair–Chuirn bealach. This latter bealach is called Lon na Cailliche (*Lon na Kyle-yicha*, The Old Woman's Marsh), and it sure lives up to its name.

Across the bealach, a direct ascent would take you onto the craggy ground of Beinn a' Chuirn's western front. Circumvent the crags on the left. An old fence climbs from the bealach, with traces of a wet path beside it. When the fence turns sharp left, the path continues diagonally up the hillside below the crags but soon disappears. Continue in the same direction to outflank all steep ground and reach drier, less clingy grass slopes that curve up to the Mhanach–Chuirn saddle. Continue to the ▲summit and return the same way.

If bagging △Beinn a' Chuirn on the way back, make sure you don't get into difficulty on those crags. To regain the Achaladair–Chuirn bealach from the top, as noted in Route 39a Alternative Descent, head in the direction of Beinn a' Chreachain until you can see a safe way down.

GiGi: When descending to the Achaladair–Chuirn bealach, whether from the Dothaidh–Achaladair bealach on the outward journey or from Beinn Mhanach on the return journey, recce the ensuing ascent route across the bealach. The path up to the Dothaidh–Achaladair bealach can be especially hard to find on the return trip so, on the outward journey, make a note of landmarks to aim for on the way back.

Needlepoint: Route 39b is best left for a clear day. When Beinn a' Chuirn is shrouded in cloud, navigating a curving route up (and especially down) the featureless slopes above the Achaladair–Chuirn bealach, to avoid the west-facing crags, isn't easy. Nor is finding the traverse path back to the Dothaidh–Achaladair bealach.

Chilly Willy: Provided you avoid Beinn a' Chuirn's crags, the route up Beinn Mhanach from the Achaladair–Chuirn bealach should present little winter difficulty. However, the path from the Dothaidh–Achaladair bealach to the Achaladair–Chuirn bealach crosses steep ground. If it is obliterated by snow, the traverse can become surprisingly exposed.

BEINN DORAIN

BEINN AN DOTHAIDH

BEINN ACHALADAIR

S Top   Summit

Beinn a' Chuirn

BEINN MHANACH

Route 39c The Five Beinns: All Five Bridge of Orchy Munros from Auch Farm

G3 ***** NN 317354, 21ml/34km, 2200m/7200ft M182

According to Torpedo, Auch farm is perfectly placed as the starting point for an enterprising round of all five Bridge of Orchy Munros, beginning up the south ridge of Beinn Dorain and returning from Beinn Mhanach along Auch Gleann.

As the four principals stand in a line north of the farm, each one hiding the next, their traverse has **a real sense of adventure** with ever-changing views. Torpedo grants that it's a long way (the longest route in this book!),

but he also maintains that you get nothing for nothing.

Climb the south ridge of ▲Beinn Dorain (Route 35c) then continue to ▲Beinn an Dothaidh (Route 35a), ▲Beinn Achaladair and ▲Beinn a' Chreachain (Route 37a). Return to the bealach between △Meall Buidhe and Beinn Achaladair, traverse to the bealach below △Beinn a' Chuirn (Route 37a Extension 2). Climb ▲Beinn Mhanach (Route 39b) and return along Auch Gleann (Route 39a).

8 GLEN LYON

Glen Lyon is the longest and arguably **the most scenic glen in the Southern Highlands**. Sandwiched between the grassy hillsides of the Lawers Range and the Glen Lyon Horseshoe, it eschews dramatic mountainscapes for **a serene, sylvan, soothing beauty**.

The glen road gives access not only to the 'backside' of the Lawers Range, which separates the glen from Loch Tay to the south, but also to six more Munros on its north side. Four of these form the Glen Lyon Horseshoe, AKA the Carn Mairg Range after the reigning peak. The broad, undulating ridge that links the summits is as green and uneventful as you'd expect hereabouts, yet a trampers' delight for these same reasons (Route 40a).

The two remaining Munros stand in isolation further up the glen.

Easygoing Meall Buidhe would not look out of place on the Horseshoe (Routes 44a and 44b), but Stuchd an Lochain asserts a more rugged individuality with a craggy corrie that is by far the glen's most (only!) imposing mountain feature (Routes 45a and 45b).

North of the Horseshoe, not strictly in Glen Lyon itself, stands another isolated mountain that brings this section's Munro tally to seven. Not that 'isolated' is an adequate description of the celebrated Schiehallion, which positively revels in its solitariness as the most distinctive and aloof mountain in the Southern Highlands (Route 46a).

There is nothing around here for the likes of Terminator, but others will find in Glen Lyon and its environs plenty of easy excursions to keep them cheerfully occupied.

CARN GORM

An Sgorr

Viewed from the path up Meall nan Aighean

The Glen Lyon Horseshoe:

▲**40 Carn Mairg** 91 1041m/3415ft (OS 51, NN 684512)
Carn Merrak. A direct translation from the Gaelic gives the meaning Cairn of Pity or Regret, which supposedly commemorates a plague that decimated Glen Lyon in the seventh century. A more likely meaning is the less poetic Rusty Cairn, from the Gaelic *Meirg*, perhaps referring to autumn colours.
△Meall Liath 1012m/3320ft (OS 51, NN 693512)
Myowl Lee-a, Grey Hill
△Meall a' Bharr 1004m/3294ft (OS 51, NN 668515)
Myowl a Vaar, Hill of the Top

▲**41 Meall nan Aighean** 169 981m/3218ft (OS 51, NN 694496)
Myowl nan Yun. *Aigean* means Abyss in Gaelic, but the most likely meaning is Hill of the Fawns or Heifers, from the Gaelic *Agh*.

▲**42 Meall Garbh** 186 968m/3176ft (OS 51, NN 647517)
Myowl Garrav, Rough Hill
(not to be confused with its namesake ▲32)

▲**43 Carn Gorm** 103 1029m/3376ft (OS 51, NN 635500)
Carn Gorram, Blue Cairn
△An Sgorr 924m/3032ft (OS 51, NN 640509)
An Skorr, The Peak

Peak Fitness: No change to existing Munros and Tops since original 1891 Tables, although until 1997 Meall nan Aighean was known as Creag Mhor (not to be confused with ▲24 in Glen Lochay). The older name is now accepted as belonging to a crag on the south-east hillside. Meall Luaidhe (*Myowl Looy-a*, Lead Hill, NN 656510), the furthest gentle swelling south-east of Meall Garbh's east top, was an additional Top until 1981.

The four Munros of this **Queenly Quartet** link arms to form a crescent-shaped horseshoe around the hamlet of Invervar at the heart of Glen Lyon. They are rounded, grassy, virtually featureless mountains whose summits are little more than mammary highpoints on a sweeping, plateau-like ridge. That doesn't sound very appetising, we admit, but if the sky is blue and you have a desperate need to head towards it and wander lonely as a cloud to your heart's content, there is no more inviting place in the Southern Highlands.

Paths and terrain are excellent, escape routes are numerous and high bealachs enable the summits to be bagged in a single expedition for barely more upward effort than an ascent of Ben Nevis.

The Glen Lyon Horseshoe isn't everyone's bowl of porridge, but on a good day there are worse things to do than stravaig this **great rollercoaster in the sky**.

CARN MAIRG

MEALL NAN AIGHEAN

Glen Lyon

Above Inverinain (Route 31d)

GiGi: Recalcitrant local estates have attempted to come to terms with the passing of the Land Reform (Scotland) Act 2003 by regimenting access to the mountains. Chesthill Estate, on whose land the Glen Lyon Horseshoe stands, has a history of restrictive practices towards walkers. The huge iron gate at the start of the walk was padlocked until the Act enforced free access.

The estate now wishes you to walk the horseshoe in a clockwise direction and stay out of all corries and glens! You are not obliged to heed such advice, but do take note of stalking restrictions (main season:

mid Aug to 20 Oct). Further information available on local notices or at:
    website: www.chesthill.com
    tel: 01887-830312

Similar stalking restrictions (main season: 20 Jul to 20 Oct) also apply at Lochs Estate, on whose land Meall Buidhe and Stuchd an Lochain stand. For further information, check local notices or contact the estate manager at Managed Estates:
    email: me@managedestates.co.uk
    tel: 01786-462519

No stalking takes place on a Sunday.

Route 40a The Glen Lyon Horseshoe from Invervar
G1 **** NN 666483, 11ml/17km, 1450m/4750ft M205

This is a tricky route to rate as opinions on it vary widely. We award it four stars for when the sun's out, but ambitious ramblers might well give it more, while rock jocks will certainly give it less. And if you go on a dreich day, you've only got yourself to blame.

If you think four Munros in a day is pushing it, check out the Shorter Options on Page 209. The four-bagger can be tackled in either direction but we prefer an anti-clockwise circuit. In this direction, routefinding is easier, views are improved (the morning sun is behind for views ahead, while the afternoon sun is behind for views back), the initial ascent is less tiring and the day ends beside the tumbling Invervar Burn.

Meall a' Bharr

CARN MAIRG

Coire a' Chearcaill

MEALL NAN AIGHEAN
SW Ridge

Begin at Invervar, 8ml/13km from Coshieville at the foot of Glen Lyon. There's a hidden car park a short distance down a side road just before the telephone box. From here, cross the glen road, go through the iron gate opposite and follow a Land Rover track up through woods on the right-hand (east) side of the Invervar Burn. Leave the track at the first telegraph pole beyond the woods for an excellent path that climbs Meall nan Aighean's south-west ridge around the rim of Coire a' Chearcaill (*Cyarcle*, Circle).

At a levelling at a height of 530m/1740ft, the path crosses a wider stalkers' path that comes up from the right, crosses the ridge and heads left to a dilapidated hut in the bowl of the corrie. The stalkers' path begins on the approach track 20 metres before the telegraph pole and makes an equally excellent alternative ascent route but, as it stays below the crest

of the ridge, we prefer the ridge path for the views.

The path continues up the broadening ridge almost all the way to Aighean's summit and makes for **a pleasant, well-graded ascent**, despite the disconcerting sight of the Horseshoe skyline stretching away to the west, *behind* you, as you climb north-east. The path becomes indistinct higher up but, thanks to short grass underfoot, it is hardly needed. The rocky ▲summit is the further away of two rounded tops, being 7m/23ft higher than its neighbour and the most easterly point of the day.

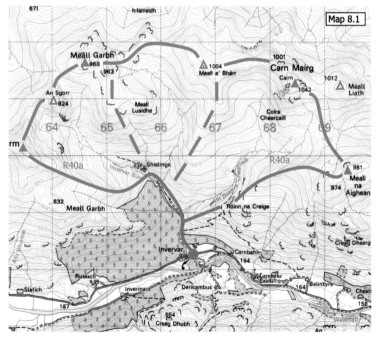

Looking west on
Meall a' Bharr

Now the skyline traverse proper begins as the route heads north across a broad, hummocky saddle to a second pair of rounded tops, the leftmost of which is Carn Mairg, the highest summit in the range. The right -hand rise is ΔMeall Liath, which Top baggers will wish to visit, but the main path gives it a body swerve. On descent to the saddle you'll pass a spring at NN 692497, worth noting on an otherwise waterless ridge walk that, on a hot summer's day, will help sweat off a few kilos as part of a calorie-controlled diet.

Approaching Carn Mairg, the obvious way up would appear to be via the saddle between it and Meall Liath, but the path cuts left below the skyline to ascend a grassy rake and find a more congenial way up through the boulderfield that skirts the ▲summit. As the northern view opens up, Schiehallion looks attractive across a deep intervening glen, but that's for another day.

Heading due west at last from the

summit, **the great sweeping spine of the Horseshoe draws you onwards**. A short descent leads to a stony crest and a broken fence that will be with you all the way to the next Munro and beyond.

The path finds good going on grass below the crest, crosses a small rise (Point 1001) and reaches the most effortless part of the walk, along the great flat top of ΔMeall a' Bharr. We don't care what Terminator says about the Glen Lyon hills, this section of the Horseshoe gives **a superb sky-high stravaig**. NB Beware older maps that misplace Meall a' Bharr's name away from the summit.

Coming off the end of Meall a' Bharr, a short descent leads to a long, 864m/2835ft-high bealach, at the far end of which is the only lochan *en route*. An even shorter ascent then takes you up Meall Garbh, the third rounded, twin-topped Munro of the day. Go over or around the east top to reach the 5m/16ft higher ▲summit (west top). The former Top of Meall

Luaidhe lies c.800m off-route south-east of the east top.

One more Munro to go. Halfway down to the next bealach, the fence of which you have now become so fond bears right towards Loch Rannoch and should be left to its own devices. Across the bealach, a direct ascent of the final Munro of Carn Gorm is blocked by the nuisance of a peak that is ∆An Sgorr.

Despite its name, and the presence of a few crags on its far side, this is a tedious little excrescence. This late in the day you'll probably be cursing the extra 80m/250ft of ascent and descent required to surmount it and reach Carn Gorm beyond.

For those who so wish, and we make no moral judgements on the matter, there's a bypass path around the thing. Unless you're a Top bagger, we suspect you'll take that path. For some reason, it is well-worn.

Carn Gorm is the most westerly and shapely Munro of the group. F-Stop has even managed to produce photographic evidence that makes it look pointy from some angles. Even so, and even if you choose not to go over An Sgorr, the 290m/950ft pull from bealach to summit is the stiffest of the day. The true ▲summit lies 100m beyond the trig. pillar and rewards with the best views on the whole Horseshoe.

To descend, take the path that curves down Carn Gorm's south-east ridge and around the upper boundary of a large forestry plantation into the upper glen of the Invervar Burn. After reaching the stream, stay on the near bank and, hidden around a corner, you'll find a bridge (NN 659494) that gives access to the approach track on which you began the day. On a sunny (midge-free) summer's evening, the stream is very inviting.

Meall a' Bharr

CARN
MAIRG

MEALL
GARBH

GiGi: The curious, beehive
-shaped building passed
near the start of the walk
is a restored eighteenth
century lint mill, used to
mechanise the production
of linen from local flax.
Worth a look.

F-Stop: As befitting the last Munro of the day, Carn Gorm
is a good place to take a break, and the best views in the
range encourage the (in)activity. There are **terrific views**
not only up and down Glen Lyon but also across it to the
Munros of the Lawers Range and Tarmachan. Above all,
though, it is the view back along the Horseshoe, all the
way to Meall nan Aighean 5½ml/9km away, that will leave
you gasping at what you have just achieved.

MEALL GARBH

An Sgorr

Summit

E Top

From CARN GORM

To MEALL
NAN AIGHEAN

Invervar

Needlepoint: You'd think that good
paths, and a broken fence along much of
the ridge, would make the route fairly foul
-weatherproof, but don't bank on it. The
path is sometimes indistinct and
sometimes non-existent. Just one wrong
turn in the featureless landscape and you'll
discover why the Horseshoe has earned its
navigational notoriety.

Chilly Willy: The main winter problem on
the Horseshoe is not technical difficulty
but length. These are benign winter
mountains that in normal conditions give a
good yomp in the snow, but in less than
perfect conditions you can easily run out
of light. Bagging the four Munros as two
pairs, as described under Shorter Options,
will give two less fraught days out.

Route 40a Shorter Options M205

CARN GORM

MEALL NAN AIGHEAN
SW Ridge

If you run out of time or energy after climbing the first two Munros, you can always leave the last two for another day. After bagging ▲Meall nan Aighean and ▲Carn Mairg, there is a choice of at least three ways down, all of approximately equal length.

Round trip: 7ml/11km, 1000m/3300ft.

(1) Return to the saddle between Carn Mairg and Meall nan Aighean and traverse easy ground above Coire a' Chearcaill to regain the approach route on Aighean's south-west ridge.

(2) From the saddle, descend right (west) into Coire a' Chearcaill to reach the old hut noted above and the start of the stalkers' path back to Aighean's south-west ridge.

(3) For a change of scenery, head west along the skyline from Carn Mairg to Meall a' Bharr and descend the latter's pathless but easy south-west ridge to the Invervar Burn path.

To bag the last two Munros as a separate expedition, walk up the Invervar Burn path to an old corrugated tin hut and shielings marked on the map at NN 656498, then head straight up the hillside to the summit of ▲Meall Garbh. From there, continue to ▲Carn Gorm and descend as described previously.

Round trip: 7ml/11km, 1080m/3550ft.

▲44 Meall Buidhe 248 932m/3058ft (OS 51, NN 498499)

Myowl Boo-ya, Yellow Hill (not to be confused with its namesake ▲184 in the Western Highlands or with ▲6 Beinn Bhuidhe)

MEALL BUIDHE
SE top
Meall a' Phuill
Loch an Daimh
Stuchd an Lochain N Ridge

Peak Fitness: Meall Buidhe has been a Munro since the original 1891 Tables, although until 1921 it was called Garbh Mheall (*Garrav Vyowl*, Rough Hill). That name is now applied only to the lower north top. The south-east top was an additional Top until1981.

I f the rounded summits of the Glen Lyon Horseshoe are unremarkable, the similar but lower summits to their west, punctuating little-visited country on the north side of the upper glen, are even more so. Only Meall Buidhe heaves itself over the magic 3000ft mark to attract humankind to its lonely top. Yet we like Meall Buidhe. While some mountains flatter to deceive, unassuming Meall Buidhe scorns

vulgar ostentation... which only makes its amazing summit even more remarkable. We're talking about **one of the best viewpoints in the whole Scottish Highlands**.

The most effortless ascent route begins at Loch an Daimh (*Loch an Daff*, Stag Loch), near the head of Glen Lyon (Route 44a), but you can also reach the summit from Loch Rannoch to the north (Route 44b).

rough ground and burgeoning afforestation on the lower slopes make this option increasingly less than enticing.

You are more likely to be seduced by the track's right-hand branch, which continues up the glen of the Allt Sloc na Creadha (*Owlt Slochk na Cray-a*, Stream of the Claypit) to the right of Garbh Mheall. It runs for a further 1ml/2km to the foot of Coire nan Cnamh (*Corra nan Crav*, Corrie of Chewing, probably of cattle), between Garbh Mheall and Meall Buidhe.

From the end of the track, the summit of Meall Buidhe can be seen for the first time at the head of the deep-cut corrie. Climb the corrie's less steep left-hand side, seeking patches of grass and game paths to ease the heathery going (Garbh Mheall did not earn its Gaelic name for nothing). Higher up, the terrain improves and the angle eases as you cross the shallow bowl of the upper corrie to gain Meall Buidhe's ▲summit.

Needlepoint: In foul weather, this is a much more straightforward approach to Meall Buidhe than Route 44a. There is no path in Coire nan Cnamh, but by following the stream to the skyline you should stay on target.

Chilly Willy: Routefinding may be easier on the Rannoch side of the mountain than on the Lyon side, but Coire nan Cnamh faces north-west and holds snow longer than the south side of the mountain, making the Bridge of Gaur approach a tougher winter proposition. Be prepared to encounter steep snow slopes.

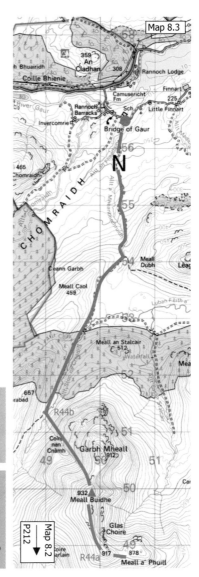

▲**45 Stuchd an Lochain** 197 960m/3150ft (OS 51, NN
483448) *Stoochk an Lochin*, Peak of the Lochan
△Sron Chona Chorein 927m/3041ft (OS 51, NN 493445)
Strawn Chonna Chorrin, Nose of the Meeting of the Corries

STUCHD
AN LOCHAIN

N Ridge

Loch an Daimh

Peak Fitness: No change since 1891 Tables.

Stuchd an Lochain stands isolated
on the south shore of Loch an
Daimh, directly across the water from
Meall Buidhe. On approach it looks no
more exciting than any other grassy
heap hereabouts, but for once those
featureless lower slopes conceal not
one but two notable mountain
features, which is two more than the

other six Munros in Glen Lochay can
muster between them.

Screened from roadside
rubberneckers around a corner of Loch
an Daimh, the Stuchd's northern flank
rises in one great sweep from the
lochside, so gouged by glaciation that
little of it remains except **an
enormous craggy corrie** (Coire an

Lochain, *Corra an Lochin*, Corrie of the Lochan). The summit perches on the corrie rim, high above a circular lochan and at the apex of a rousing north ridge that must surely have been sited in Glen Lyon by mistake.

By far the best approach to the mountain, despite an over-worn path, is from the lochside via the corrie rim (Route 45a), perhaps returning down the north ridge (Route 45a Alternative Descent). If you need a quick tick or an easier way up in winter, an approach from Glen Lyon, via the Stuchd's dreary southern slopes, will save a minimum of effort but forego a maximum of scenery (Route 45b). During the stalking season Lochs Estate wishes you to use Route 45a (see Page 203).

Route 45a Stuchd an Lochain from Loch an Daimh
G2 *** Route Rage Alert NN 500463, 5ml/8km, 650m/2150ft M218

We award the route three stars in honour of its enthralling summit, although the lower section of the approach path is currently in such a dire condition that you may have difficulty appreciating the mountain's true potential.

Begin at Giorra Dam, at the end of the minor road to Loch an Daimh, at a height of 400m/1300ft on the north-east side of the mountain. Take the hydro road to the left side of the dam and the continuing vehicle track along the south shore of the loch (it goes to a boathouse).

Just around the first right-hand corner (NN 509461), leave the track for a path that climbs the hillside to Point 887. This highpoint on the east rim of the Coire an Lochain is sometimes called Creag an Fheadain (*Craik an Aiten*, Waterpipe Crag), although that name more properly applies to crags overlooking Loch an Daimh lower down.

The hillside up which the path climbs is littered with broken crags that complicate routefinding. The route indicated on the estate's road-end notice board ascends directly from the boathouse. We advise you to keep to the path.

To find the easiest line, it makes a shallow rising traverse into a steep, grassy depression, which it then climbs to the skyline. Unfortunately the path is so infuriatingly boggy that you'll spend more time off it than on it.

It may be only 400m/1300ft to the skyline but it's a stiff pull, alleviated

GiGi: Stuchd an Lochain has a unique claim to fame in that it was the scene of the first ever recorded ascent of a Munro, around 1590. The bagger, more (in)famous for abducting ladies and executing Macdonalds than for his hillwalking exploits, was Colin 'The Mad' Campbell of Glen Lyon. Although some say you have to be mad to climb mountains, Colin's excuse was to stalk game.

only by views back down the green trough of Glen Lyon. Patience, patience. Your reward awaits.

The path reaches the skyline on the east ridge of Point 887, not far below the top. Note this point for the return trip, to ensure that you leave the ridge in the correct place to avoid the crags. A broken fence along the crest of the ridge accompanies you up the last couple of rises to Point 887's domed top, where the view finally opens up over Coire an Lochain to the Stuchd's summit on the far rim. Now the fun can begin.

With good going underfoot at last, the path turns south-west to follow the old fence around the broad, curving corrie rim and across a shallow saddle to the rounded Top of ▲Sron Chona Chorein. The actual highpoint of the Top, should you wish to visit it (and why wouldn't you?), lies 30m back

from the highest point reached by the fence. There's also a bypass path that contours below the Top to save a modicum of ascent and re-descent (only to be used on the return journey, obviously). A glance at the map will show that the Top is well-named, with corries indenting it on all sides.

Turning west, **a spacious stravaig** leads onwards along the rim of Coire an Lochain, between its abysmal depths and the sharply contrasting southern hillside, which falls away tamely to Glen Lyon (Route 45b). In the dark craggy recesses of the inner corrie nestles Lochan nan Cat, which unlike its namesake on Ben Lawers (Route 31a) forms an almost perfect circle and doesn't look at all like its eponymous beastie. Beyond another shallow saddle, steeper slopes rise to the Stuchd's distinctive half-dome ▲summit.

STUCHD AN LOCHAIN

Sron Chona Chorein

STUCHD AN LOCHAIN

F-Stop: The summit view would be almost as good as that from Meall Buidhe, if Meall Buidhe weren't in the way. The attractive mountain basin seen below, hemmed in by steep hillsides at the head of Loch an Daimh, rivals the head of Loch Lyon as the least trodden country in the Southern Highlands.

STUCHD
AN LOCHAIN

N Ridge

Sron
Chona
Chorein

Lochan
Na Cat

Needlepoint: There are occasions in the Scottish Highlands when you may notice the odd spot of dampness in the air. In such conditions, both the boggy ascent path and the steep Alternative Descent via the north ridge are best avoided. If the mountain is in cloud, the main navigational problem is on the return trip – finding the correct place at which to come off the east ridge of Point 887, to avoid the crags below. Our advice is to wait for better conditions – the path really is purgatorial when wet.

Chilly Willy: When the path is obliterated by snow, the ascent to the east ridge of Point 887 can become surprisingly steep and exposed, especially if you fail to find the easiest line. There are no real obstacles as long as you avoid craggy ground, but this is no place to learn how to use ice axe and crampons.

The steep slopes rising to Stuchd an Lochain's summit dome may also give pause if iced. Although they are no steeper than the slopes of Point 887, the adjacent drop to Lochan nan Cat certainly adds to the *frisson*. Coire an Lochain is **spectacular in winter**, but you'll obtain only limited views of the lochan itself owing to the generally convex nature of the corrie rim. Don't get over-ambitious in your efforts to peer over the edge or you may end up with a lochside close-up.

The Alternative Descent of the north ridge is naturally a considerably more difficult proposition, but when it's good it's very very good. Who'd have thought you'd find **an exhilarating little test piece** for budding Alpinists in Glen Lyon?

Route 45a Alternative Descent: North Ridge

G3 **** Zero additional mileage, 50m/160ft *less* ascent M218

Vertigo sufferers should return by the route of ascent, but anyone desirous of a tad more excitement should consider descending the north ridge to the lochside and returning along the shoreline to Giorra Dam.

Unique in Glen Lyon, the narrow and **beautifully proportioned upper ridge** is an unexpected treat. At one point it is so narrow that there is room on it for little else but the grassy path. A 'Bad Step' adds zest to proceedings, but it is pretty straightforward, so there is nothing here for followers of Terminator to get excited about.

From Stuchd an Lochain's summit, easy heath slopes descend to the Bad Step, which acts as a gateway to the narrowest section beyond. The Step is no more than a brief rocky drop, easy-angled and with little exposure. It barely even rates as a scramble, but it does require a spot of handwork (and maybe backside work). At the foot you are ushered onto a seductive section of level ridge in a terrific situation above Loch an Daimh. Its only drawback is its shortness.

At the far end, the route seems to disappear over the abyss, but the path finds a way down steep grass slopes among crags to reach wet ground in lower Coire an Lochain below Lochan nan Cat. These tedious final slopes make a disappointing end to the descent, but they are still less aggravating than those encountered on the normal ascent route. Take a diagonal route down to the lochside, then follow the shoreline back beneath the crags of Creag an Fheadain to reach the boathouse and the track to the dam.

Loch an Daimh

Stuchd an Lochain N Ridge

Route 45b Stuchd an Lochain from Cashlie

G1 ** NN 490418, 5ml/8km, 660m/2150ft M223

An ascent of Stuchd an Lochain via its monotonous southern slopes avoids both the northern crags and the northern scenery. Other things being equal, we'd say an approach from this side is for unrepentant tickers only. However, as the normal route up from Loch an Daimh to the north is eroded to distraction, a southern approach has the not inconsiderable merit of being less likely to disrupt the equanimity of the ascent party.

Park at the east entrance to Cashlie house, at a height of 300m/1000ft in upper Glen Lyon, and walk up the drive. Just before the house, a gate on

STUCHD
AN LOCHAIN

An Grianan

Cashlie

Glen Lyon

Viewed from
MEALL GHAORDAIDH

GiGi: Loch an Daimh was formerly called Loch Giorra. Following its damming for hydro-electric power in the 1950s, its waters backed up to join Loch an Diamh, which was then a smaller loch further up the glen. The combined loch is now named after the upper loch, but the dam is called Giorra Dam in memory of the lower loch. Pipelines carry water from Loch an Daimh (where Route 45a starts) *under* Stuchd an Lochain to Cashlie in upper Glen Lyon (where Route 45b starts).

the right gives access to open hillside on the right-hand side of the Allt Cashlie. Follow this stream all the way up and you'll reach the rim of Coire an Lochain near the summit of the mountain.

The first part of the ascent is steep and pathless but the going is good, on short grass beside a fence. Height is gained fast. Soon you pass the rocky bluffs of An Grianan (*An Gree-anan*, The Sunny Spot), the bold lump of a hill on the left, and enter the wide open spaces of Stuchd an Lochain's broad southern corrie. In contrast to the northern Coire an Lochain, this is so shallow, grassy and featureless that it is easy to lose your bearings in it, even on a clear day.

The going deteriorates somewhat in the bowl of the corrie, but the ground is nowhere near as boggy as might be expected and much drier than on the Loch an Daimh approach. Follow the line of the main stream up and out of the corrie and you'll reach the skyline at the rim of Coire an Lochain, which drops away on the far side of the mountain for a sudden and startling change of scenery.

If you're not sure which is the main stream, just keep heading up the gentle grass slopes and you'll reach the skyline at some point. Until then, there is zero scenic interest. Once on the rim of Coire an Lochain, with the summit dome of Stuchd an Lochain to your left (hopefully!), the Loch an Daimh approach is joined for the last few hundred metres to the ▲summit.

Sron Chona Chorein

Cashlie

STUCHD AN LOCHAIN

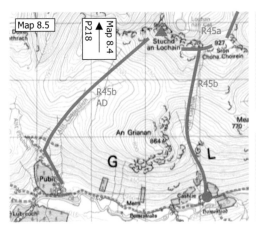

Needlepoint: In cloud, keep climbing beside the Allt Cashlie, or heading in a northerly direction, and you should reach the rim of Coire an Lochain at some point. But it will be a dismal ascent.

Chilly Willy: No problems should be encountered in the southern corrie in winter, although (as noted previously) the steep slopes of the summit dome may give pause if iced.

Route 45b Alternative Descent

G1 ** Add-on: 2ml/3km road walk

An Grianan separates Stuchd an Lochain's southern corrie from another shallow corrie (the south-west corrie), down which the Allt Camaslaidh flows to Pubil house, 2ml/3km west of Cashlie on the Glen Lyon road. Pubil is at the same height as Cashlie and is the same distance from the summit of Stuchd an Lochain.

You could climb the mountain from here, but we prefer the ascent from Cashlie on account of better going and better views on the rim of Coire an Lochain. However, providing you don't mind an end-of-day road walk back to Cashlie, a descent to Pubil allows a circuit to be made.

From the summit, descend south-west down easy grass slopes to reach the bowl of the south-west corrie. A smattering of peat bogs has to be negotiated, but aim for the Allt Camaslaidh and you should find reasonable going along its banks. In places, a streamside sheep path even encourages speedy progress over gentle terrain.

As on the Cashlie route, the hillside steepens above the road, but the going remains good. At a height of 500m/1650ft you'll come across a hydro road that makes light work of the final 200m/650ft descent to Pubil. The initial long hairpin can be shortcut. Once down, all that remains is the 2ml/3km road walk back to Cashlie.

▲46 Schiehallion 59 1083m/3553ft (OS 42, 51 or 52, NN 714547)

Sheehallion, fancifully translated since Victorian times as Fairy Hill of the Caledonians, from the Gaelic *Sithean* (Pointed Hill or Fairy Hill) and *Chaillean*. With less prudishness and greater fidelity to the mountain's shape, earlier eighteenth century mapmakers translated it as Maiden's Pap, from the Gaelic *Sine* (Breast) and *Chailinn* (Maiden).

E Ridge   SCHIEHALLION   NW Ridge

Loch Tummel

Peak Fitness: No change since 1891 Tables.

W e admit it, we don't know what to make of this ultimate mountain in *The Ultimate Guide* to the Munros of the Southern Highlands. It certainly dominates its landscape, showing up as a graceful cone from the west and an equally attractive wedge from the Queen's View along Loch Tummel to the east.

It also has a greater historical importance than most. Even the Ordnance Survey succumbs to the mountain's exalted opinion of itself and features it, uniquely, on *three* separate maps.

Yet when you climb the thing, it turns out to be nothing more than **a great muckle lump**, with a long whaleback ridge of irritating broken quartzite that rises over an irritating succession of irritating false summits. Did we mention it was irritating? But then again, there's that nice new gravel approach path, and that **extensive summit view** over loch and woodland, unhampered by surrounding mountains…

Maybe you'd better just go see for yourself. If ever a mountain needed to be climbed *because it is there*, it is Schiehallion. The normal route uses a new path to climb the gentle but bouldery east ridge (Route 46a), while seekers after solitude may wish to try the steeper but pathless north-west ridge (Route 46b).

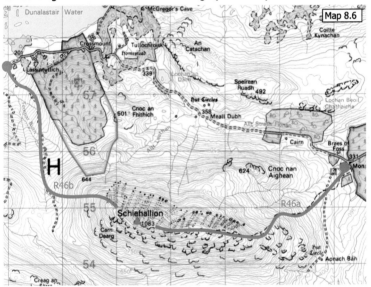

Map 8.6

Route 46a Schiehallion from Braes of Foss: East Ridge
G1 *** NN 753557, 6ml/10km, 760m/2500ft M225

From Schiehallion's conical summit, the whaleback east ridge tilts down to a shoulder, below which the ascent route begins at a car park near Braes of Foss farm, at a height of 330m/1080ft (small parking fee payable at machine). No route in the Scottish Highlands has two such contrasting halves, with **a brilliant new path** up to the shoulder and execrable going beyond.

The path was built by the John Muir Trust at a cost of £817,000, following purchase of the north-east side of the mountain in 1999. With its surface of compacted gravel, the path is such a vast improvement on the boggy morass of the old path that it rivals the new Cobbler path (Route 2a) for the access improvement it has brought.

The path crosses the moor and wends its way up the shoulder for around 2ml/3½km (3400m to be precise). It ends at a height of 830m/2720ft, at a junction with the old path and the start of the whaleback ridge. A short distance beyond here, at NN 726545, the horseshoe-shaped Maskelyne Cairn commemorates one of the Astronomer Royal's observation points.

The character of the route changes completely when you set foot on the quartzite and begin the prolonged plod up the rockpile of the east ridge, from false summit to false summit. The slope is gentle but the terrain is anything but. A stony line worn among the rocks by generations of hillwalkers attempts to find the least aggravating going but, when the rocks become too jumbled, especially higher up, you'll be left to your own devices.

As distraction, a panoramic view opens up behind over a great tranche of lowland to the Cairngorms. If motivation still falters, spur yourself on with some creative visualisation of the even more expansive view that awaits at the summit.

It is a relief to have interest rekindled at the ▲summit cairn, which is perched atop a short, narrow ridge of tilted quartzite pavement that drops in tiers of small crags to the south. Take care when you go exploring, especially if the slippery rock is wet.

After pausing to take in the view westwards, and to debate the mountain's worth, all you have to do then is descend. Some find the rubble more infuriating to negotiate on the way down than on the way up, which gives Schiehallion another claim to fame. It is a mountain on which, uniquely, you may well find yourself asking someone coming up: 'Is it far to the bottom?'

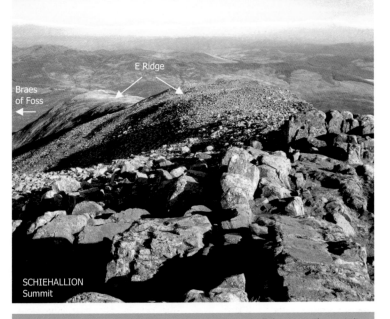

E Ridge

Braes of Foss
←

SCHIEHALLION
Summit

Baffies: Memo to self: Request JMT to extend the new path all the way to the summit.

GiGi: At NN 752553, beside the path on the right, c.200m from the gate at the end of the car park, an isolated cup-marked boulder lies among the bracken. It is thought that the many small hollows or 'cups' were carved into the rock pre-Bronze Age, between 3000BC and 2000BC, but their purpose remains a mystery. Art, cartography, ritual... you decide.

The sheep fanks further along, at the foot of the path's first steepening (NN 748547), date from the beginning of the nineteenth century, when sheep began to replace cattle as the mainstay of Highland life. Several hundred metres south of here at NN 747540, off-route along an old Land Rover track, is the hut circle of Aonach Ban (*Ernach Bahn*, White Ridge), dating from c.1500BC to early AD. Other archaeological findings dot Schiehallion's mountainsides. For further information, see www.jmt.org/east-schiehallion-estate.asp.

The new path from Braes of Foss

Needlepoint: The quartzite wasteland of the whaleback ridge is ankle-twistingly slippery when wet and ridiculously confusing in mist. Cairns and the stony 'path' make navigation fairly simple much of the time, but in thick cloud there are one or two places where you may lose your bearings, hopefully temporarily.

Chilly Willy: Quartzite? What quartzite? Schiehallion's viewpoint summit makes an even more inviting objective when the awkward rocks are under snow, so give the route **an extra star for a winter ascent**. Beginners note: ice axe and crampons are still required, of course, as is care on icy summit rocks.

Somewhere on SCHIEHALLION

Route 46b Schiehallion from near Kinloch Rannoch: North-west Ridge

G2 ** NN 690575, 5ml/8km, 880m/2900ft M225

The north-west ridge is much steeper than the east ridge and carries only an occasional path of sorts. However, a grassy Land Rover track climbs to the 600m/2000ft contour and there is much less quartzite to contend with above there.

The route as a whole takes more effort than the east ridge route and will never rival it in popularity, especially since the building of the new path, but there is not as much to choose between the two approaches as at first appears.

The track is one of two that leave the road on the south side of Dunalastair Water at East Tempar farm, 4½ml/7km along Schiehallion Road from Braes of Foss car park and 2ml/3km from Kinloch Rannoch. Park on the grassy roadside verge c.150m to the east. Take the right-hand track beside the Tempar Burn; the left-hand track goes to the farmhouse only.

The track climbs open hillside left of the stream. It aims directly for the north-west ridge then continues beyond its foot to end at a height of

SCHIEHALLION

NW Ridge

Loch Rannoch

600m/2000ft on heather slopes above the bealach to Schiehallion's west.

To avoid the heather, leave the track somewhere between the 500m and 550m contour to seek out grassy oases that give easier going. There is no one best way, but at the time of writing a small trackside cairn, if you can find it, is as good a point as any to start the ascent.

Trend back left towards the ridge then stay right of its broad crest to avoid steep heather and quartzite

rubble. Higher up, a path comes and goes and is occasionally useful, but it is easier to find on descent than ascent. Above 900m/2950ft, the average angle lessens as the ridge becomes more rubbly and rises in a series of steps.

Unlike on the east ridge, most of the quartzite is avoidable until the final boulder pile. You'll make liberal use of hands here but only for balance, so we refuse to grade the route any higher than G2.

SCHIEHALLION

NW Ridge

Needlepoint: Without an obvious path to follow, you are unlikely to find the optimal route up the north-west ridge in cloud, and keeping to the correct line on descent will require even more precise navigation. Best left for a fine day.

Chilly Willy: Apart from occasional steep snow, the north-west ridge should give no especial winter problems providing you avoid the broken crags on the left-hand side of the crest. However, the normal route up the less steep east ridge will provide a more enjoyable winter experience.

F-Stop: Schiehallion's isolation makes its summit a commanding viewpoint in all directions, although many Munros are so far away that you may struggle to identify them individually. To the west especially, the mountainside drops away dramatically

to reveal an uninterrupted view along Loch Rannoch, pointing and beckoning to the distant mountains of the Central Highlands. Those mountains eagerly await your foot-fall, armed of course with the next volume of *The Ultimate Guide to the Munros*.

INDEX

Luath Press Limited

committed to publishing well written books worth reading

LUATH PRESS takes its name from Robert Burns, whose little collie Luath (*Gael.*, swift or nimble) tripped up Jean Armour at a wedding and gave him the chance to speak to the woman who was to be his wife and the abiding love of his life. Burns called one of 'The Twa Dogs' Luath after Cuchullin's hunting dog in Ossian's *Fingal*. Luath Press was established in 1981 in the heart of Burns country, and is now based a few steps up the road from Burns' first lodgings on Edinburgh's Royal Mile. Luath offers you distinctive writing with a hint of unexpected pleasures.

Most bookshops in the UK, the US, Canada, Australia, New Zealand and parts of Europe either carry our books in stock or can order them for you. To order direct from us, please send a £sterling cheque, postal order, international money order or your credit card details (number, address of cardholder and expiry date) to us at the address below. Please add post and packing as follows: UK – £1.00 per delivery address; overseas surface mail – £2.50 per delivery address; overseas airmail – £3.50 for the first book to each delivery address, plus £1.00 for each additional book by airmail to the same address. If your order is a gift, we will happily enclose your card or message at no extra charge.

Luath Press Limited
543/2 Castlehill
The Royal Mile
Edinburgh EH1 2ND
Scotland
Telephone: 0131 225 4326 (24 hours)
Fax: 0131 225 4324
email: sales@luath.co.uk
Website: www.luath.co.uk